EMBRACING OUR ROOTS

EDITED BY RACHEL G. HACKENBERG

EMBRACING OUR ROOTS

A Barbara Brown Zikmund Reader

UNITED CHURCH PRESS

United Church Press, an imprint of The Pilgrim Press
1300 East 9th Street, Ste 1100
Cleveland, Ohio 44114

thepilgrimpress.com

Library of Congress cataloging-in-publication data on file.
LCCN: 2025930845

ISBN 978-0-8298-0442-3 (paper)
ISBN 978-0-8298-2260-1 (ebook)

Printed in the United States of America on acid free paper.

CONTENTS

FOREWORD

History is organic; it grows and flowers, it dies back and goes to seed. It needs tending, like a garden, to produce its best blooms. Sometimes it benefits from fertilizer. At other times careful pruning and even the grafting of old branches on to new stock will revive its beauty.

Barbara Brown Zikmund, "Beyond Historical Orthodoxy." *Hidden Histories in the United Church of Christ*, ed. Barbara Brown Zikmund (United Church Press, 1984), x.

BBZ
A UCC Primer

For those of us born and raised in the United Church of Christ, and those of us who joined the UCC long after the denomination's 1957 formation, it can be easy to miss the youthfulness of the United Church of Christ. For those of us who came to know the UCC in the wake of its impactful "God is still speaking" identity campaign in the early 2000s, it can be easy to overlook the efforts of our denominational elders to inform the identity of this unique Christian community in its early years.

Barbara Brown Zikmund, known to colleagues and fans as BBZ, is one of those influential denominational elders. Across a lifetime of deep theological and historical work, BBZ has shaped our UCC self-image by observing it back to us, serving as a loving mirror in which our best and worst are known for the purpose of clarifying God's call upon our collective life. Her knowledge of who we are—and *why* and *how* we came to be who we are—is unparalleled.

In recent years, BBZ and I have brainstormed how we might, from the vast wealth of historical information she has curated into books published by The Pilgrim Press/United Church Press, assemble a single resource through which that information might feel accessible to readers. (After all, not every UCCer craves a complete, seven-volume set of *The Living Theological Heritage of the United Church of Christ*.) One answer to our brainstorm, as it turns out, is a collection of BBZ's own writing. Gathered together, these selected articles and essays form an essential primer about the denomination whose theological history BBZ has championed.

To the works collected here, limited edits have been made where rules of language and grammar have changed since original publication of the materials: a comma instead of a dash (or vice versa), the use of "humanity" instead of "man," the acceptance of the singular "they," and the like. Edits and abridgments to the text are careful not to alter the original meaning. In some places where BBZ herself amended a quoted text by expanding "men" to include "women," her edits remain as marked by parentheses—a reminder of the gender dynamics in language and in church that she was actively working to shift.

BBZ was ordained in the United Church of Christ in 1964. She completed her doctoral degree in 1969. She was the first woman to teach at Chicago Theological Seminary (1975), the first woman to serve as Dean of the Faculty at The Pacific School of Religion (1981), the first woman to be elected President of the Association of Theological Schools (1986) and President of Hartford Theological Seminary (1990). She has pastored and preached, written and researched, served on a city council and keynoted General Synod. She has worked on ecumenical commissions for both the National Council of Churches and the World Council of Churches.

Many of us know BBZ from our bookshelves. Her *Hidden Histories of the United Church of Christ (Volumes 1 and 2)* are required reading for polity courses. If Louis Gunnemann—another common name on UCC shelves—was the historian of the denomination's formation, BBZ is and has been the preeminent historian of our denomination's theological identity. Her work observes the diverse ways we live out our faith; it reminds us of the roots from which have grown our varied expressions of church; and it offers up knowledge to inform our ever-evolving (one might say, "still speaking") denominational identity. BBZ reminds us—individually, congregationally, and denominationally—that we are a work in progress, and in this we find hope.

Engaging Our Roots is arranged for reflection on our Christian faith, our UCC identity, and our ongoing Christian commitments to one another. These themes emerge from BBZ's writing in denominational publications across decades of UCC life. Discussion questions are offered throughout this collection by the editor, whether for use in a course or book group or personal enrichment. The original sources for these collected writings are cited as the first footnote to each article; additional footnotes in the articles were included in the original publication. God and BBZ know, *Engaging Our Roots* is only the tip of the deep iceberg of wisdom that BBZ has poured onto paper across the years. In the Archives of Women in Theological Scholarship at The Burke Library (Union Theological Seminary, New York), the volume of BBZ's papers from 1958 to 2001 exceeds 120 boxes.

The following four introductions of BBZ speak not only to her material work but also to her character and impact, and on this topic, I am lost for words except to offer my awe. BBZ has a graciousness and fortitude that I marvel to witness, and I am humbled to curate her words in this modest collection. The highest gratitude we can express for BBZ's wisdom, I think, is to faithfully and actively exercise our faith, to embrace the diversity of our shared UCC identity, and to choose our covenantal commitments to one another over the polarizing divisions by which the world increasingly brands itself.

—Rachel G. Hackenberg, *Editor*

BBZ

Laying a Foundation That Is Built to Last

Successful construction projects require an expert surveyor to assess the necessary angles, contours, and boundaries of a site before creating a plan. This is critical because it reveals potential obstacles that will delay or even prevent completion. Over the past four decades, Barbara Brown Zikmund (a.k.a. BBZ) has served as the master surveyor on the landscape of theological education. Her skills were nurtured in her love for the Church, shaped by her historical curiosity, and fueled by her passionate commitment to secure places for women on the landscape of theological education. In a 2009 interview she stated,

> I came along in the mid-seventies when more and more women were becoming visible leaders in religious communities. I began to see that this was a moment in history when some of the past patterns of leadership were going to change dramatically and that I was at the right place at the right time. I began to feel that working in theological education was a very special calling that I could respond to.[1]

And respond she did! BBZ was the *first* woman to join the faculty at Chicago Theological Seminary, the *first* woman Dean of

1. Dallas (Dee) A. Brauniger, "Antoinette Brown Women: Finding Voices" PDF, September 2009, page 15.

the Faculty at The Pacific School of Religion, the *first* woman President of the Association of Theological Schools (ATS), and the *first* woman President of Hartford Theological Seminary. Amid all those "firsts," she developed and sharpened specific skills that opened doors for other women to enter, challenge, and transform theological education.

This historic threshold brought BBZ into the firmly established world of male-centered angles, contours, and boundaries in the theological academy. It was held in place by a "vertical plumb line," sustained by the gravitational pull of hierarchy and privilege. It was counterbalanced by a "leveling plane" of deeply rooted policies and practices that resisted reform or change. Yet she brought the optical tool of the "prism" to refract light and begin to shift those very angles, contours, and boundaries toward more equitable alignment.

One of many notable accomplishments during her four-decade career was BBZ's leadership on the Women in Leadership in Theological Education Project. In 2010, the ATS journal *Theological Education* presented its findings that included her summary of the research. This groundbreaking endeavor examined and assessed the state of theological education through the lenses of women who served as CEOs and CAOs. Their panoramic views and untold stories convicted and challenged the traditionally held analyses of leadership in theological schools, creating new questions that are still being answered today.

At the nineteenth-year celebration of the Women in Leadership initiative, BBZ offered these words of affirmation and support to her sister "surveyors" in theological education:

> "I remember when I started thinking about becoming a president," she recalls. "Everyone is watching. Can she do it? But just meeting expectations is a trap. Women need to

> claim their creativity to set new goals and stretch leadership in many directions."[2]

As one of the participants at that empowering event, I offer my sincere gratitude for the courageous examples and life-giving insights of Barbara Brown Zikmund, who has laid a foundation for women in theological education that is built to last!

—Julia M. Speller, PhD
Member of the UCC Historical Council
Professor Emerita, Chicago Theological Seminary

2. Eliza Smith Brown, "Celebrating ATS Women in Leadership: In Praise of Pioneers . . . and Mentors," Theological Education. The Association for Theological Schools, March 2016 (ats.edu).

BBZ

Making History Accessible

My first mistake was addressing her as "Dr. Zikmund." I had been invited to work on a project she was leading, the *Living Theological Heritage of the United Church of Christ,* a seven-volume series documenting two-thousand years of backstory to the modern denomination. As a relative newcomer to UCC historical circles, I assumed that the typical forms of academic deference would be required. But I was wrong. Without hesitation, "Dr. Zikmund" corrected me: she was BBZ and only BBZ. None of that extra "doctor" stuff was going to be necessary.

I did not make the second mistake, which would have been underestimating her. I had earned my history Ph.D. in the early 1980s, when women were still a barely tolerated minority, and so it was not hard to imagine the grief that BBZ and her pioneering generation must have endured years earlier, how much determination and intellectual elbow grease had been required to push through and receive their degrees. In fact, this is probably why my first memory of BBZ is about names and titles. Back then, as now, it really meant something for a female academic to forego the usual honorifics, to insist on just being herself. It was (and is) way too easy for the wider world to overlook a woman's accomplishments and tag her by her first name—just ask Hillary.

Clearly, BBZ was formidable. When I joined the LTH team, I saw so much to admire: the breadth of her historical knowledge, the zest for detail, intellectual curiosity and personal determination, but most of all her gift for collaboration. BBZ was not a zero-sum leader. We were, to be sure, an extremely motley crew, a mishmash of historians and theologians and pastors and archivists, most of us dug deep into our own corner of the UCC's pre-merger past. Yet somehow, around the table at our editorial meetings, she got us talking (mostly one at a time), building conversations that became, over time, genuinely ecumenical. Even more, BBZ kept us on track. The project took years, and she kept the momentum going until the last document had been scanned, the last introduction written, the last names and dates checked for accuracy. And in all of that time, filled with more than the usual frustrations, hours of academic nitpicking and more than a little denominational one-upping, no one walked away.

And somehow, in the midst of everything, BBZ never took herself too seriously. In fact, when she joined the UCC Historical Council, we began to have some actual fun. Usually at Synod meetings, the Congregational Library and the E&R Historical Society would share a booth, handing out brochures and membership forms to any passerby unwary enough to slow down for a look. BBZ changed all that. She got us into costumes. We became Samuel Sewall in a black robe and powdered wig, Antoinette Brown Blackwell in a long skirt and bonnet, Abner Jones and Washington Gladden and Louis Nollau and Joseph Rieger in nineteenth-century coat-and-tails, wandering around the exhibit hall buttonholing people and telling them our life stories. And though I can't say we changed the tide or, God forbid, made ourselves cool, we did manage to shake loose some old stereotypes. We were making history accessible, something more than endless names and dates and boredom. We showed that the past, its stories, and its people were interesting, surprising, intriguing, and even sometimes a little bit fun.

That was her mission. In the years that I saw BBZ serving on the Historical Council, the board of the Congregational Library and Archives, and so many other organizations and causes, I knew she would always bring good ideas. Her deep sense of history gave her an instinct for what was essential; like all good historians, she was not dug into the past, not worried about change. None of this is easy, especially in these days of distraction and despair. In recent years we have seen the past politicized, hijacked, and left for dead, deemed irrelevant to the demands of the present. BBZ's great gift—to me and so many others, both living and dead—was her passion for history. I am eternally grateful for that conviction, her core belief that the past, with all of its mess, contradiction and complexity, deeply matters to all of us.

—Margaret (Peggy) Bendroth, PhD
Historian of American religion
Former Executive Director, Congregational Library & Archives

BBZ

Premier Historian

Barbara Brown Zikmund, known as BBZ, is one of the premier historians of the United Church of Christ, a church she dearly loves. She believes that it is important for us to know and understand our past in order to live faithfully into our future. She has been particularly interested in lifting up the lesser-known parts of our history. She has had a particular interest in the contributions of women in the church, both their historical presence and their experience as clergy.

When I was invited to join the UCC Historical Council in 2013, I was excited to be in the presence of so many UCC luminaries, such as BBZ. When, a few years later, BBZ asked me to become the chair of the council, I told her I couldn't possibly. I didn't feel I knew enough, didn't have the depth of experience in the UCC. It was then that I experienced firsthand both the difficulty of saying no to BBZ and her incredible supportive presence.

Barbara Brown Zikmund has been a wonderful mentor to me and to so many others. I had the privilege of accompanying BBZ during the 2023 General Synod in Indianapolis. Person after person came up to her with memories and gratitude for their work together on so many different projects.

One of her most recent projects was her work on the Afro-Christian Legacy & Preservation Project. Through the amazing work started by this project, the Historical Council realized that there was an Afro-Christian denomination that had never been recognized. The UCC Historical Council recommended recognizing the Afro-Christian Convention as the fifth stream of the United Church of Christ in 2022, and it was recognized by the UCC General Synod in 2023.

All of us in the United Church of Christ owe a great debt to Rev. Dr. Barbara Brown Zikmund.

—Rev. Nancy Nollau Mack, DMin
Chair, UCC Historical Council
Board Member, Central Atlantic Conference

BBZ

Scholar, Teacher and Friend

Other writers have illuminated the substantial contributions BBZ has made to understanding our theological heritage and the groundbreaking contributions she and many ordained women have made to both church and society. I want to highlight her role in raising awareness of the Christian Church and its gifts to the tapestry that is the UCC. (The Christian Movement became part of the new General Council of Congregational Christian Churches in 1931.)

My parents grew up in the Christian Church. My grandfathers and great-grandfathers were Christian Church ministers. I shared my heritage with BBZ and noted that I was uncovering documents from those clergy forebears. She was excited. When I unearthed a large, nineteenth-century ledger filled with the handwritten minutes of the Ohio Central Christian Conference from 1829 to 1893, she exclaimed, "Rob, you have to insure it and get it into safekeeping."

I took many notes about the ordinations of my forebears and the churches they served in Ohio. The treasured volume was given to the Congregational Library for its archive of Christian Church records. In 2009, when the General Synod met in Grand Rapids, BBZ gathered a group of people interested in the story of the Christian Church in the UCC. She wanted to inspire others to discover missing records.

BBZ is my inspiration in the continuing effort to find still-missing records of the Christian Church. Recently, I found a connection between the Christian Churches in Ohio and their support in the nineteenth century for Franklinton Christian College, a school important to the Afro-Christian Convention. I am deeply grateful to my friend for proposing me as a member of the Historical Council. She has enriched my life and elevated the Christian Church story.

—Rev. Robert F. R. Peters, Jr., DMin
Retired UCC Pastor
Historian of the Christian Church tradition

SECTION I

Affirming Our Faith

Jonathan Edwards wrote passionately about love and communion with God, encouraging people to leave egotism behind: "Religion, in its purity, is not so much a pursuit as a temper; or rather it is a temper leading to the pursuit of all that is high and holy. Its foundation is faith; its action, works; its temper, holiness; its aim, obedience to God in improvement of self, and benevolence to humanity."

Barbara Brown Zikmund, "Jonathan Edwards: A Theological Grandparent," *UCC Roots*. January 5, 2019 (ucc.org).

We Are Saved by Christ's Mystery

At Christmas each year, Santas, reindeer, Christmas trees, holly, angels, ribbons, etc. overwhelm us. People talk about putting "Christ back into Christmas," but most of us have no idea what that would mean. Who is Jesus Christ?

The Preamble to the Constitution of the United Church of Christ states that Jesus Christ is the sole Head of the church. Jesus Christ is Son of God. Jesus Christ is the savior of humanity. What does that mean?

Christians have been debating about Jesus Christ for a long time. In the first century, the disciples of John the Baptist came to Jesus and asked him to tell them who he was. He did not answer directly. He told them to look at his work and decide for themselves.

After Jesus was crucified, and his disciples became convinced that he was still alive, controversies about the nature of Jesus Christ raged. Christians said that, although a truly human Jesus really did die on the cross, Jesus Christ was from and of God from the very beginning. He had overcome death and was still alive with God.

Thinking about Jesus Christ in this way was not logical, but it was (and still is) theological.

Jesus Christ is just like all of us, fully and completely human, and at the same time Jesus Christ is fully and completely Divine. When the UCC says that Jesus Christ is the sole head of the

Barbara Brown Zikmund, "At Christmas, we affirm the mystery of Christ's humanity, divinity." December 13, 2003 (ucc.org).

church, it affirms this mystery. We are not simply followers of some great human leader or prophet, we are a people actively engaged by and saved through the mystery of incarnation ("God in the flesh"). We live under the headship of Emmanuel ("God with us").

On Christmas Day in Rome in the year 448 CE, a Christian Pope named Leo I preached a sermon on the "two natures of Christ." Most of us don't think of Pope Leo I as part of UCC history, yet he is. He reminded those fifth-century Christians (and he reminds us) that in Jesus Christ "each nature continued with its own characteristics, but so close a unity was established between them that the divine was inseparable from the humanity and the human indivisible from the divinity."

Every Christmas, as we sing carols about this mystery and light candles in wonder, it is appropriate to ponder what it actually means to say that Jesus Christ is the "sole head" of the United Church of Christ.

Further Discussion: We affirm the mystery of Christ's humanity and divinity—indeed, we are saved through that very mystery, as BBZ notes. How do we reflect this mystery in our church life?

We Continue Christ's Life

During Lent, Christians are challenged to think about the life and death of Jesus. Being able to explain the importance of Jesus Christ is something we all need to do—especially at Easter. Conflicting Christologies—explanations about the significance and importance of Jesus Christ—have led to great theological controversies.

One such controversy developed among German Reformed leaders on the mid-nineteenth-century North American frontier. Led by John W. Nevin (1808–1886) and Philip Schaff (1819–1893), two seminary professors at the German Reformed Theological Seminary in Mercersburg, Pennsylvania, they argued for a Christocentric, rather than a bibliocentric, theology. Although Nevin and Schaff were not very popular at the time, in recent years many members of the UCC have come to appreciate the insights of Mercersburg Theology.

Nevin and Schaff focused upon the incarnation—the concept that God out of love for humanity redeemed humanity—rather than saying that human salvation was dependent upon the atonement, the suffering and sacrificial death of Jesus.

They did not deny the atonement but wanted to interpret it in the light of the incarnation. They accentuated the sacramental practices in the Church, encouraging faithful Christians to be part of the

Barbara Brown Zikmund, "19th-century Mercersburg theology emphasized sacramental, Christ-centered church," *Past as Prologue*. April 13, 2004 (ucc.org).

church—the ongoing body of Christ—rather than promoting revivalistic preaching designed to bring about individual conversion.

Nevin wrote that the incarnation itself (the fact that God was in Jesus Christ reconciling the world) brought about union between God and humanity. The incarnation was not simply a framework for Christ's atoning death; the incarnation was God's plan that through union with Christ, humanity would find union with God.

This view of incarnation led to a rich ecclesiology, or theology of the church. Mercersburg ecclesiology argues that the church is the continuation of Christ's life on earth through the agency of the Holy Spirit. The church is not simply a collection of believers, but in the church, Christians are mystically united with Christ into one spiritual whole as part of the mystical body of Christ.

Therefore, Mercersburg Christology and ecclesiology are extremely ecumenical. The church is one and Christian unity in Christ is a divine gift, never a human accomplishment. Inspired by Mercersburg theology, the UCC continues to call itself a "united" and "uniting" Church.

Further Discussion: In the sacraments (communion and baptism), we participate in the church—which is the body of Christ. As the living body of Christ, filled with the Spirit, how do we continue Christ's "united and uniting" work?

We Are Empowered in Christ

Late sixteenth-century England was filled with controversy about the best way to reform the church. Those who had been influenced by Swiss Protestant reforms in Calvin's Geneva considered the Church of England too "Roman" and too hierarchical. Many of them wanted to "purify" the church, writing long theological tracts arguing for political and ecclesiastical change. Known as Puritans, they believed that it was possible to reform the church and the government from within.

More radical church leaders disagreed. To them the authority of bishops and the rule of government over the church were unbiblical. Their solution was to "separate" from the corrupt church and form congregations of believers grounded in "covenant and fellowship." By the 1580s, small groups of Separatists began going into exile in the Netherlands, rather than obey the rules of the Church of England.

Robert Browne (c1550–1633) was living in the Netherlands when he published "A Treatise of Reformation without Tarying for Anie" in 1582. He was the first English church leader to set forth the idea of the church as a covenantal community, although it is not clear that that idea had any direct impact on later Congregationalism. However, his argument for action without waiting was significant.

Barbara Brown Zikmund, "Radical 16th-century Separatists: Church is a community." October 13, 2003 (ucc.org).

Browne began by trying to affirm the theoretical legitimacy of the monarch and the Parliament as civil authorities. However, he was quick to state that, in practice, the magistrates were "worse than beasts," because they "pull down the head Christ Jesus to set up the hand of the Magistrate." In Browne's thinking, civil authorities had absolutely no power over the church or its pastors, because the church was ruled by Christ. Therefore, since the magistrate had no authority over the church, clergy did not need to wait for the government to institute reforms. Browne was impatient with moderate Puritan reformers, who argued for tolerance in the face of difficulties. "How then dare these men teach us, that any evil thing is tolerable in the church?" when, for Browne, right church government could remedy everything, immediately.

Although Browne himself actually went back to the Church of England later in his life, his argument that reforms are the responsibility of the people and not dependent upon political or ecclesiastical authorities was revolutionary. Then and now, he challenges all Christians who see the need for change to embrace reform without "tarrying." If Jesus Christ is the head of the church, there is never a time when the people under Christ are prohibited from acting.

Further Discussion: What is the freedom of each UCC congregation to reform itself (including its governance structure, its physical property, its education and worship routines, its mission)? We believe that Christ empowers the church to reform itself; what causes the church to "tarry" in its response to this holy empowerment?

We Discern God's Word

German Congregationalism began when German peasants in the late eighteenth century accepted the invitation of Catherine the Great, ruler of Russia (1762–1796), to settle in the southern Volga River basin. Catherine granted German immigrants special rights and privileges: they were allowed to speak and teach German, live in self-governing towns, and be exempt from military service in the Russian army. For almost 150 years, Germans in Russia flourished.

Unfortunately, in 1871, when the modern nation of Germany was established, Russian rulers began to get nervous about the Germans living in Russia. In the mid-1870s, they terminated the special privileges of German villages and instituted compulsory military service. This prompted thousands of Russian-Germans, many of whom had never lived in Germany, to leave Russia. Some went back to Germany, some went to Argentina, but most immigrated to the United States.

The American frontier in the late nineteenth century led many Germans from Russia to settle in the upper plains states and the far West—the prairies of Iowa, Nebraska, the Dakotas, and the central valley of California. Once relocated, they did what they had done in Russia. They established self-governing towns and German language schools. They continued the kind of spirituality

Barbara Brown Zikmund, "German Congregationalism," *Past as Prologue*. August 16, 2006 (ucc.org).

they had cultivated in Russia, organizing and promoting churches that followed Congregational principles.

Germans from Russia were biblically focused, fiercely independent, and wary of denominational authority. They organized to train clergy, to support a superintendent, and to publish needed educational and liturgical resources. Their *Katchismus* (Catechism) did not begin with the Law (like Luther's Catechism) or with human need (like the Heidelberg Catechism), it began with a question about the Bible: "How can one discern that Holy Scripture is God's Word?"

Over time they developed a relationship with the American Home Missionary Society (AHMS was a missionary agency of American Congregationalism) that led to formal cooperation between the German General Conference, Congregational State Conferences, and the National Council of Congregational Churches in the United States. In 1927 this long-standing relationship was formalized. Today a small number of German Congregational Churches are part of the United Church of Christ.

Further Discussion: What is your answer the *Katchismus* question, "How can one discern that Holy Scripture is God's Word?" Compare this question to the first questions of the Evangelical Catechism ("What should be our chief concern in life?") and of the Heidelberg Catechism ("What is your onlycomfort, in life and in death?"). How are these three catechism questions asked and answered throughout the UCC's activities?

We Are Called to Gospel Living

Most of us agree that being a Christian is more than a set of beliefs; it requires right action. Furthermore, Christian action, we think, ought to be informed by the Bible. Yet in the history of the church, Christians have read the same Bible and sometimes ended up justifying radically different actions—especially related to questions of war, race, gender, and sexuality.

The nineteenth-century U.S. struggle over slavery is a case in point. Many northerners condemned slavery, whereas southerners supported it. The Rev. James Pennington, who was born a slave in 1807 in Maryland, escaped to become one of a handful of well-educated African American clergy serving Congregational churches in Massachusetts and Connecticut. He was active in the anti-slavery movement.

Pennington, like many black Christians, struggled to have faith in a God who could permit slavery—who could make such a "serious blunder" in the order of things. He could not imagine how a wise and good God created a world with the evil of slavery. "If I am deceived here—if the word of God does sanction slavery, I want another book, another repentance, another faith, and another hope! I speak very reverently, and from a deep and mournful reflection," he wrote.

Barbara Brown Zikmund, "Sometimes biblical texts present conflicting messages." February 13, 2003 (ucc.org).

In his struggle with this issue, Pennington came to believe that slaveholding was "condemned by the general tenor and scope of the New Testament." Why? Because the system of slavery produced great cruelty. Look at the actions supported by slavery, he preached. "If we could calculate the amount of woe endured by ill-treated slaves, it would overwhelm every compassionate heart." Such actions did not "agree with the gospel." No text in the Bible, he insisted, sanctions cruelty, or mangling, or imprisonment, or starvation, or torture. Therefore, Christians must ask other Christians "by what authority they have done these things and continue to do them."

Pennington thought that Northern Christians had "a right to refuse communion with American slaveholders as Christians." "My brethren," wrote Pennington, "the question is fully settled with me; I hope it is with you."

There are issues in our time where biblical texts present conflicting messages that divide Christians. Like Pennington, we might do well to ask, what is the "general tenor and scope of the New Testament?" How do various beliefs relate to actions? And what actions are in keeping with the whole message of the gospel?

In the end, the answers to such questions probably are more important than any of the prohibitions or practices found in particular biblical texts.

Further Discussion: In the United Church of Christ, we "affirm the responsibility of the Church in each generation to make this faith its own in the reality of worship, in honesty of thought and expression, and in purity of heart before God" (per the Preamble of the UCC Constitution). How do we practice this responsibility "in keeping with the whole message of the gospel"?

In 1963, as a member of North Congregational Church in Stamford, Connecticut, retired MLB player Jackie Robinson was awarded the "UCC Churchmanship Award," and gave a short speech at the Fourth General Synod in Denver, Colorado. Robinson told a story: "A young African American boy who did not know about segregation showed up at an all-white church wanting to go to Sunday School. When he was told it was impossible, he sat down on the steps and started crying. Soon God came by and asked the boy what was wrong. When the boy told him, God sat down and began to cry, too. Why? Because God had been trying to get into that church for many years."

Barbara Brown Zikmund, "Remembering Our History: Jackie Robinson," *UCC Roots*. November 2017 (ucc.org).

Going Deeper

We Are Called to Be the Church

Why the church? How do ordinary folks understand the church, this church, or any church? Our theologies claim that the church is not like other organizations. We speak of the church as the "body of Christ" or "God's people." The church is a human institution which incarnates Divine purposes. It is our church—but it is God's church.

If the question is put, "Why the church?" there are two basic answers: "There is no good reason for the church" *or* "The church should exist because . . ." Those people who believe that the church should exist will give various reasons, reflecting diverse theologies and experience. We shall examine them in a moment.

But folks who say that there is no good reason for the church express what might be called a secular view of the church. For these persons the church is unimportant. At one time in human history there may have been good reasons for the church, but those reasons no longer exist. The secularist sincerely believes that progress, or history, or science, or psychology, or philanthropy, or government have assumed, transformed, explained away or superseded the roles and functions once held by the church. The secular view says that we have outgrown the church in the maturity of modern civilization.

Barbara Brown Zikmund, "Why the Church?" *New Conversations: Volume 3/Number 3*, ed. Theodore H. Erickson, Winter 1978/79 (United Church Board for Homeland Ministries).

Most secularists view the church as harmless and irrelevant. Weak people lean on the church, but strong people never bother. If you need church for some personal reason, that is your choice—but there is really no need for the church in contemporary life.

One variation of the secular view, however, does not even remain neutral about the church. There are folks who insist that the church is worse than irrelevant; it is bad, evil or demonic. The church is a crutch keeping humans from fulfillment. The church is distorting scientific truth and misleading innocent people. In American church history this has not been a popular stance, but it continues to flourish in many places.

Most people do not hold a secular view of the church. We may wonder sometimes about the beliefs and practices of some groups that insist they are right and everyone else is wrong—but few of us will write off *all* church life as irrelevant or consider churches demonic. We believe that the church should exist. We offer answers which reflect our assumptions and our experience in church. We defend the church with four types of arguments:

ANTIQUARIAN VIEW

First, there is the *antiquarian* view of the church. This is a position that is impressed with history, continuity and longevity. It believes that the church *was*, therefore it always *should be*. If so many people over so many centuries have built so many buildings, worshipped so many times, trained so many ministers and healed so many hurts, then it must be good. A personalized version of the antiquarian position asserts that the church must exist because my grandfather founded it, or my mother was baptized there, or my children were married there, or I will be buried there.

This argument from history is significant. We do need to honor past efforts, events, and leadership. Tradition is a powerful ingredient in the human story. We take comfort in our confidence that traditions will last. We are told to be good stewards of what has been given to us.

But does the church of our ancestors deserve to exist simply because it is the church of our ancestors? This is not a theoretical question! Hundreds of small congregations across our land are struggling with the question of institutional viability. It is painful to allow a particular church (with its unique history and place) to die. It hurts to recognize that because something has *been* is not reason for it *to be*.

Yet, how many times do we hear the words "we've always done it that way" in our churches? It is easy to chide others who approach problems with an antiquarian mentality—but all of us lapse into this reasoning at times. We have our sacred traditions. We become defensive about change. We do indeed subscribe to the antiquarian argument.

PRAGMATIC VIEW

Second, many people support church work and church organizations with a *pragmatic* view. Sometimes the pragmatists may be confused with the secularists, but they are not the same. The pragmatist is not ambivalent or in any way negative about the church. Church is a good thing! It is good for me. It is good for my family. It is good for my town, my country, my world. Something this good deserves to exist and it gets my support.

The pragmatic perspective is very practical. Look at the record. The church works. It is supportive of persons. It helps families. It is useful in our society. Where would we be without it? The church is a means for mobilizing some of the best aspects of human nature. It channels our energies. It uses the talents of good people and it does good things. In American society the voluntary church has been and continues to be an aggressive agent for change. Churches are able to respond to needs more directly and quickly than government. Churches do not get bogged down in red tape.

Also, the pragmatic view values the church as an effective deterrent to anti-social behavior and excessive power. The church provides moral guidance. Through its teaching, but more significantly through its practice, it supports the common good. In its educational role it forms and clarifies values. It teaches and models altruism. In so doing, the church plays a decisive role in controlling criminal and anti-social behavior. One of the problems in contemporary culture, argues this defense of the church, is that people do not know right from wrong. We need the church, says the pragmatist, to raise up people and teach them the ways of the Lord. The church is in the best position to do this essential task.

Finally, there are pragmatic supporters of the church who may not even have a personal religious stance, or consider themselves religious people. They are not believers, but they are enthusiastic about the church. Regardless of belief, the pragmatist supports the church because it is a "good cause." As with many good causes, the individual may not have a personal need for its resources, but the *cause* deserves everyone's support. Many good and dedicated church folk, even active leaders, may have a pragmatic view of the church. They belong because the church is a positive force in their world and the church needs their support.

Of course, there are those pragmatists who join the church only out of selfish and self-serving motives. They think it is the thing to do! For social status, political credibility or informal influence they need to associate with the "right" church. But most of those who make a pragmatic defense of the church are not that crass. They simply believe in churches as important and powerful institutions which have a right to claim their time and money. All of us subscribe to a pragmatic view in some form.

PERSONAL VIEW

Third, there is the *personal* view. "I want the church to exist for me," is the essence of this argument. For these people, the church should "be" because of what it has been *to them*. The church is personally important because it has provided help in a time of need.

This defense of the church is often rooted in thankfulness. There was a time when the church made a difference in the life of a loved one, or a time of personal crisis. There is almost an "I owe it to the institution" attitude wrapped up in a sometimes-blind loyalty to the church. The church made a difference on one occasion and therefore people should continue to work for its future as an act of gratitude. If the church did not exist, how would one be able to give thanks?

Implicit in this personal position is a hidden thought that "I might need the church again in the future." And it is usually followed by an assertion that "you might need it also." The personal concern that people, particularly individuals, need the supportive structure and community provided by the church is fundamental to this thinking.

Sometimes the personal view of the church is very specific: "I like the building"; "I like the pastor"; "I enjoy the music." The church in one particular time and place impresses a person so much that everything must be done to preserve that situation. This loyalty often results in favoritism and petty arguments within the church. We all know people who leave a particular church when a specific aspect of its life that is important to them is changed. The church has value, goes this argument, only when "it serves my needs, or meets my tastes."

Of course, some people have a personal loyalty to the church which is more subtle. These are the folks who will defend the church because they have the habit. . . . "I've always gone to church." "I wouldn't know what to do without church in my life."

For these people church is part of the woodwork of their world. They are unable to, and even frightened at the prospect of, change. The church should exist because, if it did not, "my habits would be upset and I would be unhappy." Obviously the discipline of regular church life is part of a balanced Christian existence, but there are folks who are literally "hooked" on church. They sometimes focus upon one or two basic features of the church. They will tolerate all sorts of radical and disruptive changes, as long as certain sacred things remain: maybe it's the building, or the 11:00 A.M. Sunday service, or the order of certain prayers, or the Tuesday circle, or the annual bazaar. Whatever it is, it is very important, and it embodies their personal loyalty to their church.

Another variation of the personal view is one which understands the church as a basis for family or ethnic identity. We all know churches that are like closed corporations—everybody knows everybody and everyone is related to everyone else. This is the ultimate family church. Likewise, in certain places the church functions as a gathering spot for "my people," "my racial or ethnic group." Here the church is important as the preserver and nurturer of special traditions and sub-cultures. If the church does not do this, people are fearful that minority heritages will be lost and minority people will have an identity crisis. Churches exist to support *our* people, to help us understand ourselves, to preserve special histories—therefore, they must be retained.

And finally, the personal view also insists that the church should be a place of likeminded folks. The church should be filled with people who "believe what I believe, who stand for what I stand tor, who support and reinforce me in my convictions." Obviously it is fair to say that the church ought to exist to bring Christian believers together in mutual support. The weakness of this position is that sometimes there is no room for differences within the church. Instead of open dialogue and mutual exploration, closed groups congratulate themselves that they are not like other folks. All differences of opinion, interpretation, or confession are subdued. Often rigid criteria are set up for church membership. Obviously some common understanding of the faith is necessary for any church to exist, but a highly personal understanding of the church leads to chaos and fragmentation if every person tries to find a church home perfectly in tune with individual beliefs. In the final analysis an extremely personal view of the church undermines the nature of the church itself. These are the results of a *personal* view of the church.

CORPORATE VIEW

The *antiquarian* view, the *pragmatic* view and the *personal* view of the church have been with us for many centuries. Recently, however, there has emerged a new fourth argument for the church. In some ways it combines several aspects of these classic perspectives, but it is shaped by specifically modern trends. This is the *corporate* view of the church.

To avoid confusion, it must be pointed out that the word "corporate" is used here in a new way. Much religious writing focuses upon the communal or shared nature of authentic church life. We celebrate the corporate nature of the body of Christ, or the people of God. We contrast the community of the faithful with highly individualistic views of religion. Christianity, we insist, lives only with the context of shared corporate worship. Where two or three are gathered together in Christ's name, God is present and that is the church. One cannot be a complete Christian alone.

Presumably all churches are corporate in the first sense of this word. But there is another meaning of the word "corporate." In recent history there has emerged an organizational pattern of church life built upon the capitalistic economic system.

Fundamental to our economic welfare is the corporation, which the dictionary defines as a body of persons granted a charter legally recognizing them as a separate entity having its own rights, privileges and liabilities.

Although variations of this more legalistic definition of corporation certainly existed in the high Middle Ages (when the church was the "priesthood" enjoying sacred immunity), the full development of a corporate institutional style of church organization had to await the unique circumstances of our American religious experience. On the American scene, churches have become voluntary institutions patterned after the corporation or company. . . . The historical movement towards religious toleration and the eventual separation of church and state made churches "voluntary associations." Unlike their European counterparts, American churches learned to exist as organizations among many organizations, societies, clubs and groups. And out of this milieu there has emerged an institutional or corporate understanding of the church. The church deserves to exist, goes this defense, because it is an organization with specialized professional resources needed by society and individuals. Although this perspective might be described as a variation of the pragmatic view, it needs to be treated separately. Implicit in the corporate view of the church are some important assumptions about its organizational health and character, not simply its impact.

The corporate view of the church becomes most visible in American history by the late nineteenth century. It is directly related to what some scholars have called the rise of professionalism. Early in the 1800s Americans promoted education and eventually developed a system of equal public education for everyone. With a utilitarian logic, most Americans came to believe that more education would lead to better jobs. Furthermore, a good job was one which demanded special skills and competencies. Education was the means to gain expertise and enhance one's natural gifts. Good education created the expert who knew more about something than the average person. In short, our American commitment to education (prompted by egalitarian motives) eventually produced a new form of elitism based upon knowledge and specialization.

By the late nineteenth and early twentieth century many areas of American life became "professionalized." Ordinary folks, who had exalted the capacities of the common man and woman in the era of Jacksonian democracy, came more and more to rely upon specialists. During this period the professions, as we know them today, were adapted and shaped by a Victorian middle class which wanted to earn a good living, elevate the moral and intellectual tone of society, and move closer to those slightly higher on the social ladder. Law, medicine, theology, dentistry, pharmacy and veterinary medicine became the means to these goals. Soon, many other fields of learning defined sub-specialties and founded national societies.

The resulting new model of leadership in our culture was based upon an individual mastering a professional discipline. This expert was seen as self-reliant, independent, ambitious and mentally organized. Personal life and career were combined in the professional role. Professionals jealously guarded their autonomy in the name of their freedom and obligation to serve all peoples. They insisted that the best professionals should be accountable only to themselves. Each professional followed his or her personal interpretation of the ethical standards recognized by a particular profession.

Some of this development was good. It was good for leadership, particularly leadership in the churches, to develop a more precise understanding of ministry. In other ways, however, the rise of professionalism did not enrich our lives. As the middle class increased in size and advanced the idea of education by linking it to special competencies, the average citizen became a client whose obligation was to trust the professional. Authority was not shared by the schooled and the unschooled. It came to rest in special places: the courtroom, the classroom, the hospital, the pulpit. People in these places deserved respect, and everyone thought that it was more sensible to trust the professional.

Professionalism produced a pattern of dependence. It pushed the churches to the edges of the secular world of experts by making seminary-trained clergy normative church leadership. It led to a highly institutionalized definition of the church. The result was a corporate view of the church as the place or organization which regulated and supported persons (usually men) who had special skills or gifts for ministry. . . . The church came to define itself as the organization which presented trained ministerial services to the world—following the pattern of schools, hospitals, and business corporations. Eventually the church became preoccupied with its responsibility to employ the best ministers. As professional standards for ministry increased, opportunities for lay leadership decreased. Laypersons found themselves giving the planning and important work of the church to the professionals. Soon the laity spent its energy on bazaars, church dinners and carwashes to raise more money to hire more professionals.

This corporate view of the church is very pervasive. In its simplest form, it believes that the church must provide jobs for the many committed and earnest young people coming out of seminary. In a more sophisticated version, it argues that the church offers religious services to Christian and non-Christian clients through its buildings and programs—but most importantly, through its professionals. The value of a church has come increasingly to be measured by the number of ordained, paid, full-time staff it can support. The church exists to give people the best, most competent, most professional support in their religious pilgrimage. This is the corporate view of the church.

These are four very different ways that we all defend and justify the church. If we are honest, few of us escape the power of these arguments. In fact, most of the time we support the church for a combination of reasons. It is important, therefore, that we understand the diversity of answers to the original question: Why the church?

WHY THE CHURCH?

Beyond all of this human logic, many of us believe that the church exists for some theological reasons. The church is not ours, but God's. We do not belong to a church because we may, but because we must in order to fully express our understanding of the gospel. It is so easy to lapse into pious generalizations about the church that we often do not think about their theological importance. Why the church? Only God knows why.

Out of human experience and our struggle with the gospel we *can* say some theological things about the church. I offer three thoughts in random order. **First, the church exists to enable human worship.** Worship was originally a sort of "holy gossip." "Did you hear? Jesus who was killed is alive." "Come Lord Jesus" was the shared prayer of those who heard the astonishing news. Somehow, the power of the life and death of Jesus could not be grasped alone in the quiet of one's closet; it had to be explored in community. People needed to be together, to gather around—just as in any crisis, accident, or disaster when crowds gather to gawk, to look, to share impressions, to hear the story of what happened over and over. It is our way of coping and absorbing astonishing news, and out of this process we create rumors, histories, and liturgies. The worship life of the Christian church begins at this basic level. Why the church? So that we can worship. So that we can relive, remember, recount the good news. So that we can nourish our understanding and celebrate the mysteries of God's wondrous ways with the world.

Worship is the life of the church. We worship not because the church has always worshipped (the antiquarian view), not because it is healthy for human beings to come together and celebrate human community (the pragmatic view), not because we need or want a personal spiritual shot in the soul (the personal view), and not because worship is a time to get religion from the experts (the corporate view). Worship is the communal response of all people who seek to know and experience the God revealed to us in Jesus the Christ.

Second, the church exists to enable human action. When the disciples of John the Baptist came to Jesus inquiring about his purpose and mission, Jesus responded, "Go and tell John what you hear and see: the blind receive their sight and the lame walk, lepers are cleansed and the deaf hear, and the dead are raised up, and the poor have good news preached to them" (Matthew 11:4–5, RSV). Yet historically the church has spent a great deal of energy dealing with belief and dogma, rather than action. Church history is filled with controversies about the clean and the unclean, the nature of Jesus, the real presence and the authentic church. These are not irrelevant issues for action, but many times they have drained away energy and distorted the impact of the gospel. We are a people of the Word that became flesh. The first disciples did not do theology by writing a systematic treatise; they did theology on the highways and in the villages. Why the church? So that we can enact the Gospel. So that we can embody, embrace, embroil ourselves in the new life. So that we can live a new life growing in wisdom and stature before God.

Action is the fruit of Christian commitment. Churches act, not because a church should support missionary work and spread the gospel (the antiquarian view), not because there are great human needs crying for care (the pragmatic view), not because its members once were helped, or helping makes them feel good (the personal view), not because it has trained pastoral leaders whose job is to act (the corporate view). Action is the result of taking the gospel of Jesus Christ seriously.

And finally, the church exists as a means and not a goal. In this land where churches are as common as gas stations and much of the so-called "church work" done by folks is maintenance, we need to remember that the church is a means, not an end itself. We do not worship the church. There would still be a gospel tomorrow even if all of the churches disappeared. The church is a gift which supports persons on their way to a better time, a new heaven and a new earth. Yet how often we make it a crutch. The crutch becomes more important than walking itself. We spend all of our energies to keep the church alive and lose sight of its proximate importance. Jesus came that all might have life. That is its mission.

Why the church? So that we can reach the goal. So that we can be transformed, and triumphant in a new age. So that we can live in the present, ever aware of future possibility. The church does not exist to survive (the antiquarian view), it is not justified by its good works (the pragmatic view), it is not necessarily a good church even when all its members are happy (the personal view), and it cannot rely upon clergy to do its work (the corporate view). The church lives primarily *to share* its vision with the world. It is not the church when it works primarily *to exist* in the world.

Put in another way, the church is a byproduct on the way to God's mission for the world. The gospel exists for the world, not to sustain the church. There is the comment made about ministry which laments the fact that many persons called to ministry understand their role to be captured in the biblical imagery of becoming "fishers of men"—reaching out into the sea of life to catch people with the gospel. It is not long, however, before church leaders find themselves feeling like the "keepers of the aquarium." The church ceases to be God's church when it becomes an end, instead of a means.

Why the church? There are many answers to that question in contemporary American society. Hopefully it exists because people feel compelled to worship, to act and to share their vision of God's future.

Further Discussion: How do you answer Barbara Brown Zikmund's foundational question in this essay, "Why the church?" What might be the answer for your UCC congregation? What is your highest hope for the whole denomination's answer to this question—and how might we live into that answer together?

SECTION II

Forming Our Identity

Objectively, the UCC does not make sense, because the social, cultural, and religious contrasts it contains are not a natural match. The UCC gradually came to experience unity in diversity by trusting God in Jesus Christ. But the way to unity was not placid. It was rough and uneasy at times. It is probably true to say that the story of the United Church of Christ is a story of trusting God and gradually coming to trust one another.

Barbara Brown Zikmund, et al. "Becoming One Church" in *United and Uniting: The Living Theological Heritage of the United Church of Christ*, Volume 7 (The Pilgrim Press 2005), 7.

Our Strength in Paradox

People have fussed and fretted about the identity of the United Church of Christ from its birth in 1957. Some local congregations voted to join the UCC but remained reluctant to change their name, so they simply added the UCC in parenthesis: First Congregational Church (United Church of Christ). Former Evangelical and Reformed congregations changed their names to St. John's United Church of Christ, or Salem United Church of Christ, but they often remained unclear about UCC identity. What did it mean to be part of the United Church of Christ?

When strangers asked UCC members to explain the United Church of Christ, they often went through a denominational genealogy: Christians merged with the Congregationalists, the German Reformed Church united with the Evangelical Synod, Afro-Christians united with Black Congregationalists, and eventually these "streams" came together to form the United Church of Christ. Or they would explain how the United Church of Christ was nurtured by the worldwide ecumenical movement. Or they would emphasize what the United Church of Christ was *not*: it was not Unitarian, it was not the Christian Church (Disciples of Christ), it was not part of the conservative denomination known as Churches of Christ.

In 1982, as the UCC approached its twenty-fifth anniversary, Scott Libbey insisted that we *did* have an identity, but we did not

Barbara Brown Zikmund, "The UCC is Paradoxical," *Past as Prologue*. July 27, 2007 (ucc.org).

know what it was because it was wrapped up in ten paradoxes. He invited UCC leaders and members to see their paradoxical commitments as strengths. The United Church of Christ was not an "either/or" denomination, it was "both/and." Libbey wrote:

> We are a deeply rooted people—and we are an uprooted people.
> We are churches—and we are part of the church.
> We respect and honor individual integrity—and we are committed to responsible community.
> We are free and we are bound.
> We strengthen our own churches—and we give ourselves to others with diaconal abandon.
> We cherish particular traditions—and we welcome independent diversity.
> We are fiercely denominational—and we are explosively ecumenical.
> We are firmly Bible-centered—and we are openly Spirit-directed.
> We find grace in the gifts of the Sacraments—and we find the gifts of grace within the secular.
> We are intentionally local—and we are responsibly global.
> We value personal piety—and we strive for public justice.

In the twenty-first century we might add one more paradox. "We believe that God has spoken—and we believe that God is still speaking." We are the United Church of Christ.

Further Discussion: Can you identify some of the above paradoxes in the life of your UCC Association or Conference? How do these dichotomies strengthen the UCC's impact in the world?

Our Structural Tension

Most UCC church members know about the importance of local freedom and autonomy in Congregationalism and how crucial soul liberty was to the Christian Movement. People assume that the creation of our present UCC covenanted ministries structure carries on traditions from the CC part of our history. But that is only partially true.

Congregational and Christian congregations did not create national denominational structures until after the Civil War. During their early years they did not even think of themselves as denominations. Yet Congregational home mission boards, building societies, and educational entities regulated and monitored local congregational life rather tightly. By the 1950s, many of the agencies of the Congregational Christian Churches were far more centralized and hierarchical than the national bodies of the Evangelical and Reformed Church. Some observers suggest that the anti-merger Congregationalists who resisted the formation of the UCC in 1957 may have been more worried about strengthening the central authority of their own overbearing mission boards, than they were trying to avoid the rather gentle patterns of oversight in the E&R Church.

Furthermore, the Evangelical and Reformed Church, which was itself a blend of various governance patterns officially organized

Barbara Brown Zikmund, "Centralization and Decentralization," *Past as Prologue*. November 28, 2006 (ucc.org).

according to presbyterial polity, was not as centralized as many Congregationalists thought. Oversight of pastoral leadership, worship and doctrinal standards was rooted in local settings.

The Evangelical Synod of North America, especially before it united with the Reformed Church in the United States in 1934, was almost more congregational than the Congregationalists. Local pastors in the German Evangelical *Kirchenverein* (founded in 1841) were elected by a majority vote of a congregation. Lay elders ran their churches. Proud of their autonomy, individual churches quickly accepted the challenge to secure their religious freedom and liberty against the encroachments of synodical preachers and foreign synods. The whole system was extremely decentralized.

Today, as we talk about which traditions will "win" if the United Church of Christ moves to a more centralized governance system, we must be careful. Decentralization and centralization are deeply embedded in *all* of the historic traditions within the United Church of Christ. Our task is to find new ways to use these traditions to meet contemporary challenges.

Further Discussion: When have you heard the UCC ethos of "congregational independence" (or decentralization) used to defend a church's choice to disengage from denominational life? How do the traditions of decentralization *and* centralization enable the UCC to be responsive to the world today?

Our Faith in Action

Many of us know how irritating it can be when so-called religious people make pious statements about "beliefs" which seem to have no impact upon their lives. We also know how inspiring it is to meet someone whose faith bears fruit in action. For this reason, we all need to know more about a UCC theologian named Béla Vassady.

Béla Vassady was born in Hungary and befriended by James Isaac Good, longtime leader in the German Reformed Church. He came to the United States in 1922 and two years later graduated from Central Theological Seminary in Dayton, Ohio. He served several Ohio Hungarian churches and also attended Princeton Theological Seminary. After returning to Hungary, where he finished his doctorate in 1927, he joined the theology faculties of the Universities of Pápa, Sárospatak and finally Debrecen. When asked about his "American experiences," he praised American activism. America "taught me to turn my classroom theology into action theology at times when deeds truly spoke louder than words." He sought to embody "so-called American activism in European garb."

During the Second World War, he was a highly published professor and a well-known Hungarian Reformed church leader. As the war progressed, he became involved in relief work in

Barbara Brown Zikmund, "Hungarian theologian appreciated 'American activism.'" April 13, 2003 (ucc.org).

Budapest. After the war his theological writings and his ecumenical experience led him back to America. Here, although he was invited to teach at the new Fuller Theological Seminary, its conservative theological stance could not affirm his ecumenical commitments. Finally in 1952, after a brief time at the University of Dubuque, he joined the faculty of Lancaster Theological Seminary, serving there until his retirement in 1973.

Béla Vassady was deeply involved in the formation and development of the World Council of Churches. As a mature theologian within the United Church of Christ, he often spoke of the church as both a beachhead and a bridge. As a beachhead, the church bears witness to God's truth. It is a prophetic critic involved in a ministry of "holy maladjustment," challenging society by confronting it with God's judgement. At the same time the church is also a bridge, testifying to the inclusiveness of Christian love. The church as bridge is "a fellowship of forgiven and forgiving sinners, proclaiming the good news, offering God's saving pardon to those who are ready to accept it."

In these times of high rhetoric and questionable actions, Vassady's theology calls us to remember that Christian "acts of holy nonconformity" must always go hand in hand with "deeds of reconciliation."

Further Discussion: Can you envision the ways in which the United Church of Christ ministers in society as "both a beachhead and a bridge"? When and where does your own faith lead you to act as a bold beachhead? a loving bridge?

Our Local Authority

In 1725, John Philip Boehm was recognized as a highly respected lay preacher. Groups of German Reformed people, unable to participate in sacramental worship because there were no ordained clergy among them, asked Boehm to lead them in the Lord's Supper. Boehm resisted. He was not ordained and he did not have authority to administer sacraments. The people, however, insisted. He could do it on *their* authority.

After a time, Boehm relented and on October 15, 1725, forty people from the German Reformed tradition gathered for communion in the small town of Falkner Swamp, Pennsylvania. Later Boehm officiated at similar services in two nearby towns. Boehm was pastoral and practical. Not only did he give people the sacraments they craved, he also drafted constitutions (or "church ordinances") to help them organize local congregations.

A few years later, when an ordained German Reformed minister named George Michael Weiss arrived in Philadelphia, Boehm assured Weiss that he had no desire to flaunt the authority of the clergy. Together they approached the Dutch Reformed Church for help. With Boehm's assistance, lay leaders in his newly organized congregations wrote to the Classis of Amsterdam about their situation:

Barbara Brown Zikmund, "John Philip Boehm," *Past as Prologue*. September 12, 2006 (ucc.org).

> Good as the land is in which we live, equally sad and unfortunate is our condition respecting spiritual things, as you can easily see. It is for this reason that the simple-minded people are exposed to the greatest danger of contamination . . . therefore, we felt ourselves all the more under obligation without delay to set up a pure religious worship and to maintain it by every agency possible, in accordance with the Word of God.[1]

The letter asked the Dutch church to recognize the validity of Boehm's ministry retroactively, so as not to "injure" Reformed religion, and to ordain him. On November 13, 1729, Dutch Reformed pastors in nearby New York carried out their request. Rev. Boehm went on to found at least ten other German Reformed congregations in southeastern Pennsylvania.

Lay leadership has always been active and significant in the history of the United Church of Christ. Although UCC people value traditions, they remain flexible and focused upon the needs of church members. For this reason, the UCC Constitution insists that the "basic unit of the life and organization of the United Church of Christ is the local church" (Paragraph 9, UCC Constitution).

Further Discussion: In your local UCC faith community, what is the authority of the laity? How do congregants demonstrate agency and self-leadership as a community responding to Christ's call, rather deferring to the congregation's elected board and/or pastoral leaders?

1. John Philip Boehm, "The Consistories of the German Reformed Churches . . . to the Classis of Amsterdam" (1728), reprinted in *Colonial and National Beginnings: The Living Theological Heritage of the United Church of Christ*, Volume 3, ed. Charles Hambrick-Stowe (The Pilgrim Press, 1998), 279.

Our Passion for Theology

The United Church of Christ is a microcosm of the history of Christian theology. Although the UCC was not officially "born" until 1957, it draws upon a long-standing and rich theological legacy. A living theological heritage has shaped, and continues to support, its common life.

Unfortunately, a perception exists that the UCC is without any roots, that it is unsure about its faith. Lutherans quote the works of Martin Luther; Methodists revere the ideas of John Wesley; Episcopalians have the division of the Church of England. But members of the United Church of Christ often seem uncertain about their theological heritage and identity.

The United Church of Christ was created out of a mid-twentieth century ecumenical passion to heal the divisions of the Christian church. Its focus was on the future, not on the past. Nevertheless it has a remarkable theological and historical legacy. This volume, and others in this series, offers resources from Congregational Christian history and German Evangelical and Reformed traditions, along with many hidden histories, to leaders and members of the United Church of Christ and to the wider society. We hope that these materials will strengthen the denomination and inform those seeking a better understanding of the past and present life of the UCC.

Barbara Brown Zikmund, Introduction (excerpted). *The Living Theological Heritage of the United Church of Christ* series (The Pilgrim Press, 1995–2005).

For example, New England Congregationalism leaned on the theological insights of key English separatist thinkers in the late sixteenth and early seventeenth centuries. Participants in American frontier religion developed six theological principles to guide their Christian witness. The theological work of John Nevin and Philip Schaff shaped and reshaped the German Reformed Church. German Evangelical immigrants brought with them a theology forged by a European "church union" movement. Few people know their heritage, and when they look for more information, it is difficult to find the sources.

The Living Theological Heritage of the United Church of Christ volumes are designed to enable the United Church of Christ to recover its theological past and strengthen contemporary faith and practice. They offer the series to the churches and their members to enable them to move beyond their theological inferiority complex and to claim their heritage. . . . We hope that *The Living Theological Heritage of United Church of Christ* will enable those who are members of the UCC to find new courage to speak with pride about their UCC faith and theological inheritance and give those who are not members of the church a clear understanding of this unique community of Christians.

Further Discussion: Whose writing has significantly shaped your theology (that is, your understanding of God)? Can you identify a historical tradition or legacy that has been a root for your faith? What elements of the UCC's theological legacy are important in your faith?

A decentralized approach to theology in the United Church of Christ is both its strength and its weakness. . . . Even as we rejoice in the freedom God gives, it is difficult to trust the freedom others claim from God. In that situation we involuntarily defend our position as absolute. To quote from Prism (Fall 1987): "Responsible theological dialogue surely requires trust and respect for the freedom of others in the fellowship of God, for only then can God's truth take over in our lives and save us from 'untruth.'"

Barbara Brown Zikmund, "Refracting Yet More Light: Prism at Ten Years," *Prism* Volume 10/Number 2 (Fall 1995), ed. Clyde J. Steckel and Elizabeth Nordbeck.

Going Deeper

Our Spiritual Roots

As a united and uniting church, the United Church of Christ does not have an extremely distinctive spiritual tradition. When comparisons are made with those denominations that look back to one founder (such as the Lutherans or the Methodists) or to one movement (such as Pietism or Pentecostalism), the United Church of Christ seems spiritually weak.

This judgment depends upon how we define strength. Recent hurricane damage on the East Coast reminds us that trees with shallow or limited root structures may look strong, but they fall easily when the winds come. Only those trees with many, deep and wide-spreading roots survive.

How do you describe your spiritual roots? What are the roots of people who make up the United Church of Christ—personally, geographically, theologically, and ecclesiastically? It is important for us to ask these questions because the United Church of Christ is made up of many people who come into our church from denominations and traditions outside of those historical groups which came together to create the UCC. Raise your hand if you were not part of the UCC or its antecedent denominations in your early spiritual journey.

Barbara Brown Zikmund, "Historical Sources of Spiritual Vitality in the UCC" *Historical Intelligencer* Volume 3/Number 2 (Fall 1985), eds. Harold F. Worthley and Lowell H. Zuck. (Historical Council of the United Church of Christ, 1986), 8–12.

So . . . the United Church of Christ may be described as a people who know what it means to be uprooted and even rootless. Looking at church history we might consider some denominations "rootbound," excessively wrapped up in their own history or doctrinal position. Being rootbound, however, is not a UCC problem.

If we carry the root metaphor a bit further, many of us are uprooted. We no longer exist on our native or indigenous roots; we are grafted. We grow and flourish, but we depend upon the roots of hardy historic plants we would not even recognize. As hybrids we bring forth beautiful blossoms suitable for our times, but we know very little about the roots upon which we depend.

Before proceeding any further in my enthusiasm about roots, however, I need to be honest. As a woman in the church, I do not like some of those patriarchal roots. I have been pruned and stunted by those roots, and perhaps it is time to take a new cutting and give me and my sisters new opportunities to grow in new directions and to sink down our own roots. That is another speech, however, for another time.

As a historian of UCC life I have an appreciation for the UCC story. In spite of my experience as a woman in the church, I know that the existing roots of the United Church of Christ offer spiritual strength for our common growth. Let us examine some of the historical sources of spiritual vitality in the United Church of Christ.

Beginning with the sixteenth-century Reformation, we find that our Protestant ancestors were practical theologians. They invited Christian people to reject any idea that full discipleship was possible only for those in the priesthood or monastic life. They set forth a new vision of Christian vocation, calling each believer to ministry according to his or her gifts. They emphasized that growth in spiritual gifts was available to all.

Although early Protestant spirituality took many forms, those forms had one thing in common: an insistence upon the centrality of the God of the Bible. Individual or corporate spiritual practices were suspect apart from the Bible. Walt Bruggemann has written on covenant spirituality, saying, "in spirituality we have to do with God, not just God in general but with a particular God whose name has been given to us."[1] And this God whose name has been given to us is the God of Abraham and Sarah, the God who comes to us in the life, death and resurrection of Jesus Christ.

The God of the Bible is both sovereign and gracious. Therefore, Christian spirituality is not first of all our movement towards God, but our gratitude for God's gracious movement towards us. A spiritual relationship to the biblical God expresses itself in our "covenant spirituality." Again Bruggemann writes:

> The dominant agenda of spirituality is to keep covenant, to live in the tension between freedom and community. And this means to be attentive to God's purposes . . . God's promises, [and] to believe God's word which gives us life when other voices dim out the word, or when we seem to live in silence where no word is heard.[2]

The Bible is central to United Church of Christ spirituality.

Probably the most creative contribution of the Protestant reformation to the history of Christian spirituality comes from Calvin's treatment of sanctification. Historian of Protestant and Orthodox spirituality, Louis Bouyer, argues that although Calvin agreed with Luther that justification by faith, independent of works, was basic, Calvin also knew "that a faith that did not produce both external works and the progressive sanctification of our whole being was but an acceptance of faith and therefore

1. Walter A. Bruggemann, "Covenantal Spirituality," *New Conversations* Volume 2/ Number 3 (Winter 1977), ed. Theodore H. Erickson, 4.
2. Ibid., 6.

would not have justified us."[3] Authentic spirituality sustains a healthy tension between emphasizing the glory of a biblical God who saves us by grace and dwelling upon the obligations of a regenerate believer to grow into discipleship by that grace.

Building upon these basic concerns it is possible to describe five ways in which a spiritual legacy has been and is being nourished in the history of the United Church of Christ. Spirituality in the United of Christ and in those traditions which undergird its identity, is seen in (1) our concern for the health of the church, (2) our practice of corporate worship, (3) our understanding of the Christian life, (4) our commitment to social justice, and (5) our participation in the ecumenical movement.

OUR CONCERN FOR THE HEALTH OF THE CHURCH

Most of the traditions which came together to form the UCC have a conviction that Christian spirituality exists in community. It is literally impossible to live a Christian life in isolation. The United Church of Christ believes, therefore, that it is especially important to strengthen the church as the context for all spirituality.

Congregationalism expressed this assumption most clearly through "church covenants," binding people to walk together on their spiritual pilgrimage. Within Congregational history, lay leaders and clergy took responsibility to evaluate the witness of those who wished to become church members and to discipline those who failed to keep the covenant. In later history, covenants expressed the fellowship and obligations between congregations as well as between individuals within congregations.

German Reformed colonists also insisted upon the importance of the church; indeed, they were called "church Germans"

3. Louis Bouyer, *A History of Christian Spirituality: Orthodox Spirituality and Protestant and Anglican Spirituality*, Volume 3 (Burns and Oates, 1969), 86.

to distinguish them from some of the more sectarian groups. In Reformed history, church consistories regularly offered spiritual guidance and cared for the spiritual health of the people.

Or consider the *Kirchenverein*, that society which built a wider fellowship of clergy and lay leaders among German Evangelical churches in the mid-nineteenth century. Life was lonely out there on the prairies. The *Kirchenverein* was a network for spiritual support. In later Evangelical history, the "annual conference" spoke to the same needs. In face-to-face family fellowship, celebrating what Bruggemann calls the "corporate interiority of the sisters and brothers," energy and stamina for Evangelical faithfulness was sustained.[4]

The means by which the many traditions of the UCC are committed to the church, selecting its membership and discerning its leadership, are Spirit-led. We gather ecclesiastical councils to test the spirits. We envision a chain of leadership from the first century to the twentieth held together in an apostolic succession of the Spirit. All of our ecclesiastical history emphasizes the importance of church as the context for Christian spirituality.

OUR PRACTICE OF CORPORATE WORSHIP

In the history of spirituality, acts of worship—private and corporate—have provided a framework for spiritual life. Let us look at some of the ways in which UCC worship traditions offer spiritual resources.

The Ten Commandments regularly reminded our ancestors to keep the sabbath. Obviously, some of their zeal transformed "sabbath keeping" into a burden, rather than a gift, but this should not discredit the importance of sabbath for spiritual well-being. Our

4. Walter A. Bruggemann, "Our Heritage and Our Commitment," *Festival of the Church: Celebrating the Legacy of the Evangelical Synod of North America* (UCC Office for Church Life and Leadership, 1978), 18–19.

ancestors knew that rest from the daily routine was important. Sabbath invited every believer to develop inner resources. What would it take for us to rediscover the importance of sabbath and regular rhythms of rest in our lives today?

Within the United Church of Christ there is a wide variety of worship traditions. Early Congregationalism was non-conformist. That meant that it rejected all formal liturgy and argued for simple services of Psalm singing, extemporaneous prayers, scripture reading, and sermon. When the Lord's Supper was shared among the faithful, individuals prepared themselves carefully. Leaders of the church "fenced the table" against the unregenerate, viewing the bread and wine as spiritual nourishment only for the saints. Gradually, however, this attitude changed and the table was opened to all as a means of grace, or a "converting ordinance." Congregationalists, however, celebrated the sacrament infrequently to guard against "dumb repetition" and "meaningless familiarity."

German Reformed worship was different. Services followed a set order and preserved continental liturgical traditions. More regular communion was common, preceded by a corporate preparatory service of penitence and confession. During the nineteenth century, great arguments arose among Reformed people over the liturgy and its revisions. While many Americans embraced the simplistic worship patterns and rationalistic theologies prevalent on the frontier, the Mercersburg movement (led by John Nevin and Philip Schaff) fought these trends.

Emphasizing the ecumenical and mystical presence of Christ in the "altar liturgy," John Nevin celebrated the objective spiritual power of the eucharist. His organic incarnational theology envisioned . . .

> . . . a real life-union in the case of the believer with the whole person of Christ, through the force of which the

> vivific virtue of his true human flesh is carried over in the sacrament particularly into our persons, soul and body, by the power of the Holy Ghost, for our nourishment unto eternal life.[5]

Although Mercersburg leaders Nevin and Schaff were out of step with the frontier revivalism of their day, they preserved important spiritual insights for our use.

Worship in the United Church of Christ benefits from still other hidden histories. Because we focus upon preaching so frequently, it is important to note how those persons in the Christian Movement emphasized spirituality when describing the preparation of the preacher.

Milo Morrill wrote that the preacher was a "generator of tremendous sensations and impressions," a leader whose mind, "thoroughly awakened, was charged to the brim with Scripture, and solemnized by prayer-vigil and lonely meditation."[6] Frontier preachers needed more than "book learning." In the Afro-Christian tradition, the preacher was able to draw upon Negro spirituals, long meter hymns, rhythmic prayers, and later, gospel music to enrich the worship life of Black congregations.[7]

Every congregation in the United Church of Christ comes together for worship at regular intervals. Personal piety and Christian spirituality within UCC history is grounded in such times of shared adoration, confession, intercession, instruction, inspiration, and petition.

5. John Nevin, "Our Union with Christ," *The Weekly Messenger* (January 14, 1846). Quoted in John Hastings Nichols, *The Mercersburg Theology* (Oxford University Press, 1966), 200.

6. Milo Morrill, *A History of the Christian Denomination in America* (Christian Publishing Association, 1912), 104.

7. See Percel O. Alston, "Afro-Christian Connection," *Hidden Histories in the United Church of Christ*, Volume 1, ed. Barbara Brown Zikmund (Pilgrim Press, 1984), 21–36.

OUR UNDERSTANDING OF THE CHRISTIAN LIFE

Beyond these various convictions about the church and worship there are different descriptions of human nature and Christian living within UCC history. These also become sources for spiritual vitality in our times.

A small theological booklet, *The Faith We Proclaim*, published in 1960 as the UCC came into being, summarized the doctrinal viewpoints generally prevailing in the Evangelical and Reformed Church. Interestingly enough, it ended with a chapter not on doctrine, but on "The Christian Life."

> The Christian response to God's call in Christ is faith, which is the bond uniting the Christian to (the) Lord. Faith is an act of the whole self; it is the new orientation of one's life which accepts God's mercy in Christ, receives the sonship God offers us through (the) Son, and acknowledges God's claim upon us for . . . service.8

Furthermore, prayer is the natural expression of a life of faith. It is simultaneously the fruit and sustenance of the Christian's personal communion with God, because doctrinal fidelity is not enough. The booklet ends with some important words about living:

> The Christian life is a life of prayer and praise, of worship and work, of faith and obedience. It is personal and it is corporate. It is gift and growth, joy and sorrow, peace and struggle, actuality and hope. It is life whose source is Jesus Christ, the Way, the Truth, and the Life. It is life lived in the Spirit. It is the life of God and of brotherhood (and sisterhood).[9]

8. Elmer J. F. Arndt, *The Faith We Proclaim: The Doctrinal Viewpoint Generally Prevailing in the Evangelical and Reformed Church* (Christian Education Press, 1960), 127.
9. Ibid., 135.

Puritan piety in seventeenth-century New England would have been comfortable with those words also. Charles Hambrick-Stowe's study of Puritan devotional disciplines points out how early Congregationalism saw the Christian life as a "pilgrimage" moving towards union with Christ. Puritan diaries documented the search for assurance and the creative anxiety which opened spiritual doors along the journey to heaven. Devotional acts and spiritual exercises characterized a path of renewed repentance and fulfillment.[10]

Lines from the Puritan poet Edward Taylor reminded his soul that salvation was a process, not a one-time event:

> You think you might have more: you shall have so,
> But if you'd all at once, you could not grow . . .
> He'll fill you but by drops that so he may
> Not drown you in't, nor Cast a drop away.[11]

Keeping a diary or journal was, therefore, an important spiritual map for Puritans. Writing it, reading it and using it gave Christians strength for the journey.

This concern for living out the faith pervades all UCC traditions. It is clear, however, that for those in the Christian Movement (or Christian Connection), issues of "character, or vital piety" were especially important. Those groups of Christians . . . were vigorously anti-creedal, celebrating the right of private judgment and liberty of conscience. Christian character was the only test for church membership. At the same time, articles in the *Herald of Gospel Liberty* (the Christian Connection newspaper) repeatedly described the Christian life in more than ethical/ rational language.

10. Charles Hambrick-Stowe, *The Practice of Piety: Puritan Devotional Disciplines in Seventeenth Century New England* (University of North Carolina Press, 1982), 89–90.
11. Quoted in ibid., 198.

> The Christian life may truly be characterized as a continual prayer to God. The soul that is full of the love of God, and has come into reconciliation with (God) through faith in Jesus Christ, has no loftier ambition, no higher aspiration, no purer desire, than that of continual personal communion with God.[12]

This is a religion that "can be felt," wrote another author, but it is not "mere sensational feeling." Religion that is felt for the right reasons "is a religion that produces the fruits of the Spirit, which are love, joy, peace, long-suffering, gentleness, goodness, faith, meekness, and temperance."[13]

Even the catechisms used by our several German traditions in the UCC can be viewed as aids for spiritual growth. In brief questions and answers, children and adults learn basic Christian doctrine and form a "common mind." Although the catechetical approach to faith can function to quench the Spirit, the Heidelberg Catechism especially has provided important spiritual comfort. To remember through the catechism that "I belong—body and soul, in life and in death—not to myself, but to my faithful Savior, Jesus Christ . . . who paid for my sins, freed me from the devil, protects me in salvation, assures me of eternal life, and gives me a willing heart to live for him" was, and is, a spiritual anchor in a rough world. Later nineteenth-century Congregationalism also believed that confidence in God's loving care was at the heart of Christian living. Yet Horace Bushnell wrote that those who are properly nurtured in Christ grow up in his care, and so "remember no time when they began to love him."[14] Education

12. An 1881 quotation reprinted in *Centennial of Religious Journalism*, ed. J. Pressley Barrett (Christian Publishing Association, 1908), 201.
13. An 1885 quotation in ibid., 207.
14. Norman Pettit, *The Heart Prepared: Grace and Conversion in Puritan Spiritual Life* (Yale University Press, 1966), 216.

through catechism and Christian nurture leads the people towards spiritually satisfying lives.

Carl Schneider, historian of the German church on the frontier, reported that the pastors and elders of early German Evangelical churches visited in the homes of church members once a year. On such occasions, they inquired "whether family devotions were regularly observed, and what devotional books were used, and whether the children were properly disciplined and instructed in evangelical doctrine."[15]

In all of the historical traditions which are now part of the United Church of Christ, Christian living was strengthened by personal and corporate spiritual disciplines. Personal meditation, confirmation classes, prayer meetings, revivals, camping programs and retreat centers were (and are) means for sustaining spiritual vitality.

OUR COMMITMENT TO SOCIAL JUSTICE

It is important to recognize, however, that spiritual disciplines in the traditions of the United Church of Christ have never been escapist. Reinhold Niebuhr noted that the Evangelical Synod, which could have lapsed into irrelevant pietism, "maintained a continuous emphasis upon the spiritual as a source of the moral."[16]

The *Manual of the Southern Convention of the Congregational Christian Churches* urged all people to "make the most of their opportunities for soul culture and the development of character by reading the Scriptures, prayer and meditation, regular attendance upon church services and by giving themselves in unselfish service to their fellowmen (and women)."[17] Authentic piety and spiritual life will always bear fruit in social action.

15. Carl Schneider, *The German Church on the American Frontier* (Eden Publishing House, 1939), 213.

16. Quoted in Robert T. Fauth, "Go Forth—and Peace Be with You," in *Festival of the Church*, 69.

17. *Manual of the Southern Convention of the Congregational Christian Churches* (Board of Publications, 1953), 12.

This connection is important for me as a woman in this denomination, because too often so-called "spirituality" has held women down and justified patriarchal tradition. I agree with James Smucker, in his recent *New Conversations* article, that we need to remain open to the work of the Spirit at *this* very moment. "We are called to plunge into the world with its divisions and despair as well as its joy—and there to discover what the Spirit is saying in our time."[18] In the context of faithful community, we are promised courage in the struggle for justice and peace *and* God's presence in trial and rejoicing.

OUR PARTICIPATION IN THE ECUMENICAL MOVEMENT

Finally, every corner of United Church of Christ history recognizes the power of Spirit to provide the bond which holds us together as a church and calls us into unity with all Christians in all times and places. We see this in our many histories, but especially in the often-forgotten legacy from the Christian Connection.

Listen to these words on sectarianism from an article in the *Herald of Gospel Liberty* written in 1849: "Heresy (does) not consist in honest belief, but in a rigid, uncharitable demeanor, calculated to produce sectarian division." If we wish to dogmatize over the faith of others, who are as good and pious as we are, making individual judgment the standard of belief for others, we are heretics. We are causing division and separation. Therefore, "the people called Christians are not to be regarded as a sect. They claim to hold Christian union with all God's children."[19]

The most recent United Church of Christ efforts to actualize our commitment to the unity of all Christians in the Spirit, namely the Disciples-UCC conversations, build upon our belief that we

18. James Smucker, "Response: Christians for Justice Action," *New Conversations*, Volume 8/Number 1 (1985) ed. William McKinney, 44.
19. Quoted in *Centennial*, 129.

are called to live into spiritual unity, not simply to consolidate institutional structures. Our new ecumenical partnership with the Christian Church (Disciples of Christ) is a spiritual pilgrimage. As the Steering Committee report to General Synod XV put it, "study alone does not lead to unity. The task of embodiment is still before us as we respond to God's gift in Jesus Christ."[20]

Furthermore, in our pluralistic world, ecumenical and interreligious dialogue depends upon experiences of "Christ" which are no longer culture-bound or historically exclusive. New sensitivities to common spiritual needs and disciplines emerge as "ecumenical aids," giving us new capacities to live creatively into convergence, consensus, communities of confessions, ecumenical partnerships, and/or organic merger. Time and the Holy Spirit invite us to remember that God's ways are not necessarily our ways and that we must wait upon the Lord.

CONCLUSION

Here then is the spiritual legacy of our UCC root structure. We begin with the conviction that church is important. We relate our expression of spiritual life to corporate worship. We explore diverse ways to live the Christian life. We combine spiritual disciplines with concern for justice in the world. And we insist that authentic spirituality is always ecumenical.

. . . I hope that the United Church of Christ can discover and appreciate its unique spiritual roots. We are so open and interested in the lively resources of Catholic, Orthodox, Wesleyan and other spiritualities that at times we devalue ourselves. I offer these insights into our past to give us a new knowledge and appreciation for UCC spirituality. I know that we are only

20. Appendix 16, *Minutes of the Fifteenth General Synod of the United Church of Christ*, June 27, 1985.

beginning to unfold the unique legacy of spirituality in the United Church of Christ. I have new thankfulness for God's mysterious ways.

Further Discussion: What worship traditions have shaped your UCC congregation? How are covenantal relationships (God's movement toward us, and our movements toward one another) practiced during worship? What spiritual tools from our Christian forbears (praying, journaling, reading the Bible, etc.) shape the ways you live out your faith?

SECTION III

Provoking Our Covenant

When religious righteousness and political certainty leave little room for difference, religious and political liberties suffer.

Barbara Brown Zikmund, "The German Evangelical Theological Style," *Past as Prologue*. April 12, 2006 (ucc.org).

We Wrestle for Holy Blessings

The United Church of Christ was founded in 1957, but within ten years the "racial crisis" of the 1960s exploded the calm of many congregations. Instead of wrangling about church union, intense arguments raged over the role of the church in society. Christian social activists called for activism in the civil rights movement, while other Christians objected, withholding funds and insisting that churches ought to keep out of politics. Controversy was everywhere.

Buell G. Gallagher (1904–1978) was a Congregational Christian/UCC minister who studied at the London School of Economics and later earned a doctorate from Columbia University. In 1938, he wrote a book *American Caste and the Negro College*. He served as president of the historic African American Talladega College in Alabama, and later became president of The City College of New York. During the McCarthy era, when fear of communism threatened many civil liberties, he handled many controversies.

In 1963 Gallagher wrote that controversy is not something to avoid, it should be welcomed, even in the church. In the midst of controversy, Christian freedom and community thrive. "The only issue which is not open to controversy is whether controversy is permissible." Controversy, he argued, is "an instrument

Barbara Brown Zikmund, "Controversy is a Blessing," *Past as Prologue*. September 8, 2005 (ucc.org).

of freedom." Controversy lifts the heavy hand of forced conformity and releases creative energies. Controversy protects freedom and unmasks falsehood. (His complete article is reprinted in *The Living Theological Heritage of the United Church of Christ*, volume 7, article 18.)

How does it do this? Gallagher insists that controversy keeps a healthy balance between indifference and totalitarianism. Without controversy, differences of opinion are labeled either "matters of taste" or "treasonous betrayal." When there is indifference there is no controversy, because nobody cares and everything is relative. When totalitarian ideas reign there is no controversy, because force or compulsion allow only one acceptable position. Without controversy in government, in education, and in religion, differences are either ignored or squelched. In both cases freedoms are threatened.

Controversy is often bitter, unpleasant and worrisome, especially in the church. Yet, in spite of our desire to avoid controversy we need to heed Gallagher's message written forty years ago. Our contemporary controversies over biblical authority, abortion, evolution, war and marriage may be blessings. Blessings? Yes, because "there is no better way to protect [political, intellectual and religious] freedom than to exercise it. There is no better way to avoid conflict than to welcome the possibility of controversy."

Further Discussion: The United Church of Christ—across its congregations, its Conference and Associations, and General Synod—is no stranger to controversy. When have you witnessed or experienced a deep wrestling in one setting of the UCC? What unexpected blessings were found through the willingness to engage the controversy?

We Stretch Each Other

In 1959, when UCC delegates came together at the Second UCC General Synod, the Executive Committee adopted and presented to the Synod a statement on pronouncements. It set forth a new way of thinking about the actions and statements of General Synod and all national, regional, and local church bodies in the United Church of Christ. The statement was reaffirmed in 1969.

Pronouncements, it declared, speak only for the body that makes them, and as such, although they are morally binding, they are never legally binding on other parts of the church. "Any agency which takes a position on an issue on which views diverge may serve to evoke creative exchange of thought and may, and frequently does, serve the Lord of the Church by stimulating the mind and pricking the conscience of the Church, its individual members, and of those outside the Church as well." Yet, UCC members are often disturbed about General Synod pronouncements, arguing that no actions should be taken on issues where there is significant disagreement.

Over the years, however, the UCC has persisted in making pronouncements on controversial matters, arguing that the actions of General Synods appropriately should confront and stretch the thinking and theological work of the whole church.

1. Barbara Brown Zikmund, "General Synod Pronouncements," *Past as Prologue*. June 28, 2005 (ucc.org).

This UCC understanding of church pronouncements is unusual and confusing. It is misunderstood regularly by the media, the general public, and even by UCC members and clergy in local congregations. The Synod is not a formal representative body. It does not *speak for* the thousands of congregations that make up the UCC. It *speaks to them*. Under the headship of Jesus Christ and guided by the Holy Spirit, it challenges UCC members in local communities of faith to rethink again and again what it means to be the church. It remembers that "many, if not most, of the Church's finest hours were when it stood for what the multitude denied or decried, and that the continuing symbol of the Church's faith and witness is a cross."

Further Discussion: General Synod pronouncements, which give public witness to the conviction of the Spirit among UCC delegates at Synod, might be described as "conversation starters" with the denomination and the wider society. How does this function of the pronouncements reflect our UCC theological heritage as you understand it?

We Value Mutual Acceptance

We love our children and we want the best for them. We have jokes about the dangers of "apron strings," but it is no joke when a child is kept in a dependent relationship too long.

The story of the church is filled with relationships. The United Church of Christ came into being in 1957 because of relationships between leaders in Congregational Christian churches and the Evangelical and Reformed Church. These two denominations were themselves products of relationships—nurtured when colonial Puritans wanted to escape from oppressive relationships, when frontier settlers insisted on more simple relationships, when immigrants sought to maintain relationships, and when European union and mission efforts supported new relationships.

In our history, we have reached out through global missions to form new relationships. Yet sometimes that effort created dependent "younger churches" and made us into overly protective "parent bodies." Sometimes our missionaries failed to let God shape the church in new settings. Sometimes sending churches ignored God's mission while promoting the mission of the church. Sometimes mission boards and younger churches could not "cut the apron strings."

Barbara Brown Zikmund, "Partnership: A Different Way of Relating to Churches." March 13, 2003 (ucc.org).

The United Church Board for World Ministries saw these problems, and in the 1980s proposed a new way of thinking and talking about UCC relationships to churches around the world. The UCC committed itself to partnership—"a mutually agreed upon commitment by two or more church bodies to relate as parts of the body of Christ and to work together to fulfill the mission of Christ in the world."

During the past twenty years the UCC has intentionally cultivated Christian partnerships based upon the biblical affirmation of the unity of God's people and the call to engage in Christian mission to bring about justice. Partnership has replaced the historic idea of "one church" as the object of mission with a vision of interdependence and community.

Yet there are serious barriers to interdependence that continue to make partnership difficult, such as unequal financial resources, artificial hierarchical structures, and cross-cultural insensitivity. The characteristics of mature partnership—mutual trust, respect, acceptance and a sense of the spiritual unity of humankind and creation, are difficult to achieve. A paper written in 1988 for the UCBWM explained why. "Mutuality in mission depends on mutual acceptance and sharing; it means much more than giving or receiving because acceptance is the key to power sharing."

Further Discussion: What ecumenical partnerships has your UCC congregation formed, locally and globally? How are power and resources shared within those partnerships? What are the theological similarities—and what are the theological differences—between a mutual partnership and a covenantal relationship?

We Strive for Trust

The name "United Church of Christ" does not carry any claim to be some "super church," but tries to express a conviction that what Christians share with each other is more than what keeps them apart. In 1956, efforts were made to help local church members see the union effort as a responsibility laid on them by their church traditions. Everyone was reassured that the rights of local churches under the Basis of Union were protected.

One key event in this saga occurred in June 1956 at the Omaha meeting of the General Council of the Congregational Christian Churches. Critics of the merger process argued that the Executive Committee had made secret commitments and promises to the leaders of the Evangelical and Reformed Church. In order to reassure delegates that everything had been done in good faith and above board, the Council held an all-night session where the Minutes of the Executive Committee from June 30, 1954, to April 6, 1956, were read aloud verbatim.

The all-night session became a bonding experience and, according to Louis Gunnemann, enhanced delegate trust in church leadership thereby solidifying support for the union. Before the Omaha General Council adjourned, it voted 1,310 to 179 (with 11 abstentions) to move forward into the United Church of Christ.

1. Barbara Brown Zikmund, "Birth Pangs of the United Church of Christ," *Past as Prologue.* March 28, 2006 (ucc.org).

Two months later, in August 1956, the General Synod of the Evangelical and Reformed Church also took official action authorizing its readiness for the proposed Uniting General Synod in 1957.

As the way was finally cleared, the two bodies exchanged messages of relief and hope: acknowledging that "some good things [had] been wrought during the time of waiting" and that "in drawing closer to you in bonds of unity, we have found ourselves drawn closer to our common Lord."

Further Discussion: How does the United Church of Christ—in its congregations, Conferences and Associations, General Synod, national setting and affiliated ministries—demonstrate its conviction that "what Christians share with each other is more than what keeps them apart"?

We Celebrate the Unconventional

The Christian Movement was a grassroots reaction against traditional religion. It emerged after the American Revolution "when political liberty had been won, when churches were readjusting themselves to meet the needs of the time, when denominational rivalries were high, and earnest souls sought the realities of the Christian life." Christians affirmed the right of the individual to interpret God's truth. They insisted that Christian character—not creedal or doctrinal statements—should be the test of fellowship. They looked to the Bible to guide their faith and practice. They asserted that Christ was the only head of the church—not popes or bishops. And finally, they promoted Christian unity, rather than perpetuating denominational conflicts.

Rice Haggard (1769–1819) was a typical Christian preacher and writer. He believed that partisan labels and names should be unnecessary among "Christians." He called for tolerance, simplicity, and unity. Although he probably did not use the phrase "extravagant welcome," Haggard's desire to free the church from sectarian controversy and human self-righteousness is in keeping with the emerging vision of the United Church of Christ two hundred years later. He wrote:

Abridged from Barbara Brown Zikmund, "Christian Satire," *Past as Prologue*. May 31, 2006 (ucc.org) and Barbara Brown Zikmund, "Hospitality Is Part of Our History," *Past as Prologue*. October 25, 2005 ucc.org).

> Would to God, that those distinctions, which have so long abounded, and trouble the christian church, were vanished away, never to return! And that union, and church communion, were every where established upon the original simple principles of the gospel![1]

Christians made religion attractive and even fun. When longstanding denominations settled for stuffy and dense preaching, Christian preachers in small congregations and revivals met people where they were. They welcomed everyone. They ridiculed preaching in established denominations, insisting that "the minister who intends to drag out his days in long preaching, would better go to fighting steam, electricity, and civilization. . . . Sermons must interest, and not disgust; rest the hearer, not weary [them]. The benediction should be pronounced upon smiling hearers, and not upon frowning ones. The audience should leave the house desiring to return again rather than preferring ever to stay away."

The Christians were a small group, and after they united with the Congregationalists in the 1930s, many people lost track of them. Yet in UCC history the Christians remain an inspiration. They would be delighted with the "God is still speaking" initiative, because the Christians knew how to critique with satire and offer anyone who was put off by traditional religion an appealing alternative. May we do the same?

Further Discussion: How does the unconventional find expression in your UCC congregation? How are humor, satire, and dissent given voice in your church to promote change?

1. From "An Address to the Different Religious Societies on the Sacred Import of the Christian Name" (1804) reprinted in *Consolidation and Expansion: The Living Theological Heritage of the United Church of Christ*, Volume 4, ed. Elizabeth C. Nordbeck and Lowell H. Zuck (The Pilgrim Press, 1999)

If it is possible to sustain denominational integrity in a pluralistic world, the United Church of Christ provides an interesting case study. Its diverse history contains examples and resources that promote church unity. At the same time, its diversity highlights issues that forever divide the Christian community: theology, ecclesiology, gender, and ethnicity (including race). Only time will tell if Paul's words about seeing in part—but someday seeing face to face—will be fulfilled in the United Church of Christ.

Barbara Brown Zikmund, "Unity and Diversity," *Hidden Histories in the United Church of Christ*, Volume 2, ed. Barbara Brown Zikmund (United Church Press, 1987), 1–10.

Going Deeper

We Testify as a Diverse and Uniting Community

As we began to do the final editing on the first volume of the *Living Theological Heritage of the United Church of Christ*, I read an article in *The Christian Century* by William C. Placher, entitled "Why Bother with Theology?"[1] Good question! Why were we attempting to gather up seven volumes of theological materials from the heritage of the United Church of Christ? What did it matter?

In that article, Placher argues that "theology matters because it lies at the heart of Christian identity." Churches do many practical things (counseling, music, advocacy for social change, healing ministries), but the most (maybe the only) unique thing a church does is preach and teach about God's love in Jesus Christ (the gospel). "If our churches are only doing things that someone else could do, then, sooner or later, even our own members will begin to ask if it is really worth the trouble."

In order to stay focused on the gospel, many Christians think that they should adhere to simple Bible Christianity. But this is too simplistic. Placher reminds us that "making sense of what the Bible has to teach us is complicated business." True biblical

Barbara Brown Zikmund, "Expanding an Ecumenical Vision: Reflections on the UCC since 1957," *Prism*, Volume 21/Number 1 (Spring 2007). eds. Lee Barrett and Elizabeth Nordbeck (United Church Press, 2007).

1. William Placher, "Why Bother with Theology?" *The Christian Century* (February 2–9, 1994), 104–108.

understanding flows out of theology, a learned way of looking "at the world in all its variety." Unfortunately, most Christians, conservative or liberal, do very little theology. E. K. Chesterton once wrote that Christianity has not been tried and found wanting; it has been found difficult and not tried.

People shy away from theology because they think it is something only scholars can do. They think that pastors have more important things to do. They think that they will not be able to locate what they need to read, or understand it when they find it. People in denominations like the United Church of Christ often expend a great deal of energy on position papers related to social and political issues, but give much less attention to the intellectual (e.g. theological) foundations that undergird those position papers. Placher ends his article suggesting that "liberal mainstream" Protestant denominations must not yield to overly simple or authoritarian answers. We need to do theology, and if we don't have "anything distinctive to say, it is unclear why anyone should listen to us and even, eventually, why we should continue talking among ourselves."

The United Church of Christ formally came into being in 1957. From its birth, critics inside and outside the UCC have labeled our church theologically shallow. By the mid-1980s, several different groups began agitating to make the UCC more theologically responsible. UCC representatives in ecumenical consultations wanted greater clarity. Christians in other denominations even wondered if we were a "church," because (they felt) we lacked theological focus. There was a proposal that we should create a UCC Book of Confessions like the Presbyterians. Others lobbied for a new "Creeds and Platforms of the UCC," patterned after Williston Walker's one-hundred-year-old *Creeds and Platforms of Congregationalism*. It was suggested that the denomination ought to establish a theological commission.

I was part of that conversation. Yet some of us argued that we did not need a book of confessions, or creeds or platforms. We needed something quite simple, and, at the same time, very complex. We needed to retrieve the diverse theological heritage of our church, and second, we needed to use that heritage to help us shape a theology for these times. We recognized that even when people were aware of some of the foundations of their faithfulness, they did not know how to name them or claim them. What was needed was a way to tap the heritage of the whole church, not just official policy statements or the writings of important visible leaders.

Out of that concern was born the idea of a multi-volume library of resources that could ground our contemporary identity and nurture future theological work in the UCC. Such a collection of resources would not tell a single story, but it could become a "quarry" providing theological foundations for our common life. In the conversations of the mid-1980s, the *Living Theological Heritage of the United Church of Christ* was born. "LTH," as those of us who have worked on this project call it, gathers together in one place the theological resources that have shaped the way the UCC "thinks" about its faith. We might say that LTH contains the theological DNA of our church; it contains the genetic resources that have produced the rich diversity and theological identity of the UCC. Materials were "chosen in relationship to the contemporary life and faith of the United Church of Christ." LTH makes no attempt to document the past; rather it is driven by a vision focused upon how the church confesses its faith and passes convictions on to others.[2]

What have I learned during this twenty-year journey with LTH? How do these resources clarify my theological understanding

2. "Introduction" to the Revised Fourth Draft (April 14, 1990) of what would become the seven-volume series, Barbara Brown Zikmund, ed. *The Living Theological Heritage of the United Church of Christ* (Pilgrim Press, 1995-2005). Hereafter LTH.

and affirm my identity (and your identity) as a part of the UCC? Here I must be quite personal. I have been teaching and writing about the UCC for twenty-five years. I am embarrassed to say, however, that much of that writing and teaching has been about the years leading *up to* 1957. Many of you are like me. We are experts on UCC prenatal history—on how the UCC was born. We know its parents and grandparents, its genealogy. . . . What new insights emerge when we look at the theological journey of the UCC since 1957? I was a teenager in the Pilgrim Fellowship of Mayflower Congregational Church in Detroit, Michigan in 1957. I am not the same person I was in 1957. The UCC is not the same church either. What happened between 1957 and 2007?

OUR THEOLOGICAL ASPIRATION

At the birth of the UCC, little was said about theology. Those who led the union of the Congregational Christian Churches and the Evangelical and Reformed Church neglected and even avoided so-called "ecclesiological questions." Gunnemann later lamented the fact that the UCC embraced social activism without developing a clear "theological grounding." He felt that the UCC came up short on the "vision, time and energy for sustained theological reflection."[3] Ironically, although the subordination of doctrinal differences to the goal of Christian unity was later criticized, in 1957 the formation of the UCC was celebrated as a turning point in American Protestantism and in the ecumenical movement. People rejoiced that two very different church traditions were able to consummate church union by *downplaying* doctrine.

Unfortunately, after 1957 the passion for organizational church merger or union became less and less satisfying. By the

3. Louis Gunnemann, *United and Uniting: The Meaning of an Ecclesial Journey* (The Pilgrim Press, 1987), 27–28.

1990s some observers began to question the ecumenical nerve of the UCC. Yet, such a judgment is too simplistic. I believe that the UCC has not forsaken its ecumenical vision, rather it has expanded its understanding of Christian unity. . . . Today, the dream "that we may all be one" is rooted in how we aspire to be the church of Jesus Christ, not in how we are overcoming historic arguments and divisions, not in resolving confessional differences, and not even in our work in the world. Today, when contemporary UCC members and leaders think about the ecumenical vocation of the UCC, they often respond that the UCC is multiracial and multicultural, open and affirming and accessible to all. We claim a unity of extravagant welcome and hospitality that is much bigger than ecclesiastical structures. The UCC affirms that God "binds in covenant faithful people of all races, ethnicities and cultures."[4] . . . Oneness, unity, and ecumenism remain important to UCC leaders, because UCC leaders and members have "an ecumenism different from the traditional ecumenism that cuts across religious divisions."[5]

The UCC has an expanded vision of ecumenism. The UCC is now affirming the unity of the whole human community and the human need to be in harmony, "to be one" with creation. It continues to affirm a unity in Christ that calls Christians into closer relationships with other Christians through church unions, but it also nourishes an inclusive commitment under Christ to celebrate the oneness of humanity in the midst of human diversity. God is our Creator and God is still speaking. The UCC believes that it has found a new way to respond to Jesus' prayer "that they may all be one."

4. LTH, Volume 7, selection 11, 52–54
5. Emily Barman and Mark Chaves, "Strategy and Structure in the United Church of Christ" in David Roozen and James Nieman, eds. *Church Identity and Change* (Grand Rapids, MI: Eerdmans, 2005), 466–492

When one looks more deeply at volume seven of LTH, it is possible to see how this unity is served by activism. When the UCC is true to its theological roots (which is not all the time), its commitment to social action is not simply progressive politics. Classic social gospel theology (embraced by many educated middle class white Protestants who came together to form the United Church of Christ in 1957) had earlier promoted a very optimistic view of human nature and anticipated that Christian activism would bring in the "Kingdom of God." History, however, unfolded differently. As the world descended into two world wars, depression, and political ideologies, many church leaders and theologians struggled theologically. Human effort did not and could not bring in God's realm. UCC leaders behind the formation of the UCC lived through that period. They became "chastened liberals." They understood that Christian unity is a gift from God, not a human accomplishment.

OUR THEOLOGICAL CONVICTION

LTH volume seven shows how the UCC commitment to social activism was not a revival of theological liberalism, nor was it fueled by naive optimism about how good people can save a troubled world. The United Church of Christ repeatedly defines itself as a body of Christians responding to the redemptive love of God in Jesus Christ. The theological journey of the UCC since 1957 illustrated the ongoing UCC struggle for "justice and peace." UCC people did not imagine that their pronouncements and actions would save the world. They were Christians with a "profound awareness of the power of evil in the world, and a deep faith in the redemptive power of God in Christ." It is important to recognize how

> . . . the distinctive emphasis of the UCC on social action in church and society is not an extension of the liberalism

> of the social gospel movement which informed much of late nineteenth and early twentieth century North American Protestantism, but a reclamation of the biblical and theological conviction that Christians are called to action because they have been claimed and enabled to be agents for salvation through God's work in Jesus Christ. The UCC engages the world, because God was in Christ reconciling the world to Godself.[6]

UCC actions understood this way are not anchored in human reason or principle, or in human virtue or conscience. Rather, through faith expressed in public witness to the gospel, the church accepts (sometimes reluctantly) a divine summons to discipleship. It asks the question, "How can people of faith know the will of God so that they may do the will of God?" The United Church of Christ takes this question seriously. In its most faithful moments, it is inspired by the mystery that God in Christ loves the world, and therefore it is called to make a difference in the world. UCC efforts to make a difference flow from its faith that God has already made a difference.

This way of defining the relationship between theology and social action is difficult to sustain and explain. UCC people are caught between (1) their confession that God has done everything already and (2) their conviction that they are called to action. When they get too involved in action and lose sight of why, they are faulted. When they dwell too much on the story of salvation and fail to act, they are faulted. Theirs is a living theological heritage, grounded in faith in an all-sufficient God and prodded by the needs of the contemporary context.

6. Editorial Guidelines for Volume 7.

OUR THEOLOGICAL WITNESS

There are several new insights that have emerged out of my work on volume seven of the *Living Theological Heritage*:

First, in 1957 the United Church of Christ was theologically confident but not theologically self-conscious. UCC leaders embraced common biblical roots and accepted various theological viewpoints with an irenic spirit (open and inclusive). UCC leaders respected Christian doctrine. They could not conceive of a church without doctrine, but they focused upon what it meant to be a Christian in the world. At the General Synod in 1959, after affirming a refreshing new Statement of Faith as "a testimony, not a test of faith," the Synod adopted a document entitled the "Call to Christian Action in Society."[7]

Even more than the Statement of Faith and the Preamble to the UCC Constitution (approved in 1961), it is the 1959 "Call to Christian Action in Society" that provided the framework for the theological identity and style of the United Church of Christ. This document focuses upon what it means to be a Christian in the world. It insists that God is "ruler of all human affairs" and that humanity must live as "one family under God." It challenges the church to pray and work for change in four areas: race relations, international relations, political life, and culture. John Bennett, dean at Union Theological Seminary in New York City, wrote that although churches should not enter into partisan conflicts, they should "influence the moral sensitivities, the scale of values and the conscience of the community as a whole."

The UCC took the "Call to Christian Action in Society" seriously. In 1963, recognizing that few Blacks were part of the regularly elected delegations sent to General Synod, UCC leaders

7. LTH, Volume 7, selection 15, 80–85.

invited ten leading UCC African American clergy to attend Synod as honorary delegates (voice without vote). As the General Synod began, Ben M. Herbster, the white, newly elected president of the United Church of Christ, asked the Synod to set aside its ordinary business to face the growing "racial crisis." He reminded the delegates that members of their congregations had worked for racial justice in the abolition movement one hundred years earlier. He challenged them to carry on that legacy as followers of Jesus Christ in the mid-twentieth century. "We shall betray our Lord if we take no action now."

Ben Herbster was not a flaming activist steeped in social gospel liberalism. He was a solid German Evangelical pastor from Ohio. His words were honest and straightforward. He chided people to "uproot intolerance, bigotry and prejudice" from their hearts, he called for the end of segregation practices and structures in the church, and he challenged the UCC (local, regional and national) to take various actions to correct injustice.[8] Herbster's leadership was pastoral and biblically grounded. For this reason his call to action did not split the church into activists and traditionalists, as it did in some denominations. It simply pushed the UCC to engage the world.

Throughout the 1960s, theology in the UCC wrestled with the creative tension between traditional faith and practice and social action. Sometimes, this was done well; at other times, it faltered. People struggled to be faithful to the gospel in their local Sunday schools and congregations *and* to bear witness to God's love for the world.

By the early 1970s, the UCC was describing its theological stance as "word-in-deed theology." Gabriel Fackre, an Andover Newton professor, spoke out repeatedly about the relationship

8. Ibid., selection 17, 92–96.

between theology and action. "Evangelism," he wrote, "is the joy and task of sharing the tale of the deeds of God." It is both "telling" and "doing." Christians cannot choose between evangelistic theological witness and social engagement in the world, because evangelism that changes persons must always be companion to social action that changes structures. Christians look to God in Jesus Christ—where the deed of God is one with the word of God.[9]

Furthermore, by the early 1970s the UCC was increasingly aware that justice issues were no longer "out there." They were challenging the inner life of the church. In 1971 the General Synod passed a Pronouncement on the "Status of Women in Church and Society," affirming its belief that males and females are equal and stating that "distinctions made by society which assume an inferior-superior relationship are contrary to the will of God."[10] Even as the UCC spoke out to support the rights of women in society, it also began to think about how sexism in the church infected its theology. This was ironic. The social justice agenda, which many people assumed diminished the place of biblical theology and worship in the United Church of Christ, suddenly became the driving force for theological and liturgical renewal. By the end of the 1970s, General Synod voted that a new book of worship be developed for the United Church of Christ "using inclusive language." In 1985 the *UCC Book of Worship* was published.

Davida Foy Crabtree . . . summarized the link between social justice, theology and language:

> Language sculptures and changes the church as inexorably as flowing water carves a rock. By the words we speak we declare ourselves, we establish relationship, we

9. Ibid., selection 28, 139–146.
10. Ibid., selection 85, 461–464.

> signal our worldview and our values. In the United Church of Christ, we have begun to declare ourselves for justice—not only justice for women, but justice in our portrayal of God. Inclusive language restores right relationship with God. It saves us from outrageous idolatry and puts us in our place.[11]

OUR THEOLOGICAL EXPRESSION

Critics of the United Church of Christ continued to argue that UCC theology was merely "a series of ad hoc opinions added on to some practical concern," or that UCC theology was made up of "words used to justify positions already taken for other reasons." This might not be all bad, wrote Roger Shinn, well-known ethics professor at Union Theological Seminary. "Ad hoc theology is not entirely wrong. If God meets us in the midst of all the events of life, it is as likely that an urgent human demand will lead to a theological insight as that theology will lead to actions."[12] . . . Authors of the Leaders Box (a 1982 resource for Christian education, developed by the Office for Church Life and Leadership) asserted that there was no official theology *of* the United Church of Christ, but there was a great deal of theology *in* the United Church of Christ.

During the 1980s, two things emerged as important. First, it became clearer that UCC theology always finds expression in shared action; it is never an end it itself. The old UCC bumper sticker "To believe is to care, to care is to do" captures that assumption. This is why the UCC Statement of Faith is an unusual "creedal statement." It does not focus upon belief in God's being, rather it affirms God's actions. God calls the worlds into being, seeks and

11. Ibid., selection 31, 164–172
12. Ibid., selection 77, 411–416

judges humanity, comes among us in Jesus Christ, and empowers us through the Holy Spirit and the church. Theologically, UCC understandings of faithfulness and mission have moved away from "affirming" or "keeping" faith, to "sharing" and "acting" faithfully in interdependence and partnership with God, with others, and with all of creation. We are not always able to articulate and act on this theology, but our more recently articulated understanding of the church as the *missio Dei* (mission of God) is grounded in our assumption that God is a verb, not a noun.

Second, UCC theology has a keen appreciation for the role of paradox, ambiguity and mystery. In the 1980s, when critics lamented that the UCC was still searching for its identity, longtime Iowa Conference minister, Scott Libbey, disagreed. He told national church leaders that we had discovered our identity, but we did not know it. Why? Because it did not fit expectations (ours and others), it was not a given static thing, and it found expression in a lifestyle filled with creative paradoxes. He wrote, "I believe the United Church of Christ is a covenant community, affirming in life and faith these contradictory pulses: systolic/diastolic; breathing in and out. These are forces that appear to be counter forces but which, in fact, participate in shaping the creative surprise that is the United Church."[13]

Allen Miller, theology professor at Eden Theological Seminary for over fifty years, wrote: there is

> . . . a powerful temptation which confronts theological thinking. It is the perennial lure to sell our birthright of wonder for a mess of information. We are prone to forget that our knowledge of God, like all communication with

13. Ibid., selection 55, 312-314

> other persons, is fundamentally different from the spectator's knowledge about things.
>
> God is not an object to be known. God is a mysterious presence to be acknowledged. We know that God works through us from the center of our being. We know that, in Jesus, God took on a personal life, the like of which we know very well from being persons ourselves. Indeed, God and humanity are so inextricably bound together that it is next to impossible to conceive of one without the other. Christian theology, however, is not a statement about our feelings or of our beliefs about God. It is, rather, a confession of what God is and does for us, and in and through us.[14]

The final volume of LTH gathers clues about how UCC Christians affirm that God is with them and shows them how to engage faithfully in life in this world. . . .

The racial crisis of the sixties, the women's liberation movement of the seventies, and the theological ferment of the eighties made the UCC more theologically self-conscious. Most people who know anything about the UCC identify the UCC with social action. Yet, this UCC commitment to social issues, when it is authentic, is not anchored in human reason or principle, nor in human virtue or conscience. It is not fueled by progressive political liberalism. When the United Church of Christ works for racial justice, for gender equality, for freedom of choice, for urban renewal, for sanctuary for refugees, for economic responsibility, for the rights of persons with disabilities, for justice for gays, lesbians, bisexual and transgender persons, it does so because it is inspired by the mystery that God in Christ loves the whole world.

14. Ibid., selection 80, 427–433

It responds by taking action to make a difference in the world, yet remembering that it is only possible to make a difference, because God has already made a difference.

OUR THEOLOGICAL COMMITMENT

In 1973 the UCC Commission on Christian Unity and Ecumenical Study and Service reported that there was a "great willingness to experiment in a wide variety of ecumenical endeavors, to seek new forms and new styles, not only for their own sake, but to build greater trust, to advance the mission and to serve the deeper needs of all humankind."[15] Even as the UCC stated some uneasiness with certain aspects of the various proposals for church union generated by the Consultation on Church Union (COCU), it challenged COCU to explore "local ecumenical groupings" and to envision church union that would overcome "divisions caused by war, by racial injustice, and by discrimination against women." In 1976 it played a key role in developing an "Alert on the New Church Dividing Potential of Some Persistent Issues," pointing out the divisive nature of . . . racism, sexism, institutionalism, and congregational exclusivism. This was a major ecumenical breakthrough. It declared that church union was more than overcoming doctrinal divisions. It suggested the need to blend classic doctrinal issues of faith and order with the activist mission concerns of Christian life and work so important to the UCC.

. . . As the UCC matured, it began to speak about "oneness in Christ" in new ways. During the 1980s, as I was a UCC representative in several ecumenical organizations, I became aware of the expansive approach of the UCC to the world. Why was the UCC so open to diversity? I sought to gather up lesser-known stories and edited two volumes of *Hidden Histories in the United Church*

15. Ibid., selection 103, 569–571

of Christ to help people recognize the longstanding diversity within the UCC. As changes in United States immigration laws produced increasing diversity in church and society, the ecumenical vision of the UCC expanded.

Finally, in 1993 the UCC General Synod set forth a new way of defining "oneness." It called upon the United Church of Christ to become a multi-racial and multicultural church "binding in covenant faithful people of all races, ethnicities and cultures."[16] Such an expanded ecumenical vision was a natural extension of the UCC birthright conviction about Christian unity. Jesus prayed "that they may all be one," and, in answer to that prayer, the United Church of Christ aggressively embraced diversity as a gift from God.

What does this mean for the UCC? New racial and ethnic minority congregations were formed. Multicultural congregations expanded. Hiring practices in church agencies and offices became more diverse. Some established congregations took cross-cultural initiatives and while others embarked upon a reflection process to become more open and affirming of all people. In 2005 the General Synod passed another resolution entitled "Called to Wholeness in Christ: Becoming a Church Accessible to All." This resolution challenged the UCC "to embody the philosophy of inclusion and interdependence, embark on study and reflection activities about disabilities, disabilities rights, and ways congregations are able to become accessible to all (A2A), remove or overcome barriers to welcoming and including all people in the work and witness of the United Church of Christ." . . .

After the 1993 action calling the UCC to become a Multiracial and Multicultural church, a Pluralism Working Group produced a booklet on the meaning of pluralism. Volume seven of LTH

16. Ibid., selection 114, 652–656.

summarizes that helpful resource and quotes its preface by Michael Kinnamon, a Christian Church (Disciples of Christ) theologian.

> "Pluralism is not simply a synonym for diversity"; it accepts diversity as a source of enrichment rather than a threat. Pluralism is not the opposite of wholeness, but central to wholeness because it values particularity. Pluralism is not synonymous with tolerance, because it sometimes must say "no" to forces that limit. Pluralism involves relating to others on the basis of their own self-definition; it requires a lifestyle of dialogue; and it denies the privilege of any single voice. Pluralism is a commitment of the whole church, yet plural- ism is always lived out in local congregations. The good news is that Christ has broken down the dividing walls of hostility and is calling the church to witness to God's intended wholeness for all creation (Ephesians 2:14). Pluralism points "beyond itself to the Source of all unity and the Author of all diversity."[17]

Bill Hulteen, longtime executive of the Office for Church Life and Leadership (OCLL), described the UCC commitment to Christian unity in terms of "hospitality." Hospitality, understood here as a spiritual discipline, has to do with an abiding sense of engaging and welcoming the other, knowing that the other can be a source of insight into the ways and will of God. Hospitality is crucial given the multifaceted presence of diversity within the unity of the body of Christ. Instead of "you can't tell me," hospitality looks forward to considering and learning from and with the other. Tonalities of anticipation and humility keep pretentiousness and shallow stereotypes at bay and replace them with disciplined and

17. Ibid., 629–630

hospitable openness to the gifts of insight and conviction being offered by and coming from others.[18]

It was 1990 when the editors working on *The Living Theological Heritage of the United Church of Christ* decided to entitle the final volume, "United and Uniting." Then, Fred Trost and I worked to organize our material into eight sections within volume seven and looked for dynamic language to suggest ongoing energy. The eight sub-sections of LTH seven are:

- Becoming One Church
- Engaging the World
- Keeping the Church Strong
- Doing Theology
- Making a Difference
- Living out the Unity
- Aspiring to be a Multiracial and Multicultural Church
- Restructuring for God's Mission

According to English language usage, these section titles all use the present participle forms of verbs. English grammar books say that a *present participle* is used with the "to be" to indicate an action that is incomplete or ongoing. The infinitive form of the verb refers to a completed action, but a participle suggests incomplete action or part of an action. For example, we say "I heard the preacher speak," but, at another time, we may say, "I heard the preacher speaking." The first instance is a statement about something that has happened in the past. It is over. But when we say, "I heard the preacher speaking," the feeling is different. Some of the speaking was in the past, but the speaking continues. When

18. Ibid., selection 140, 772–776

present participles are used with the present tense, they convey openness and energy. They affirm and invite openness to change.

What is uncanny about all of these language decisions is that they were made totally apart from the UCC "God Is Still Speaking" identity promotion. We had no idea that UCC people would come to celebrate commas rather than periods and emphasize the UCC commitment to the God who is still speaking. Yet, guided by the Holy Spirit we put together a series of books entitled the *Living Theological Heritage of the United Church of Christ*. We entitled the final volume *United and Uniting*—filling its pages with pronouncements, articles, sermons, hymns and prayers that illustrate how the UCC has been and is *becoming, engaging, keeping, doing, making, living, aspiring and restructuring*.

The United Church of Christ is a work in progress. Since 1957, we have been expanding our ecumenical vision and responding to Jesus' prayer "that they may all be one." Today we say, "No matter who you are or where you are on life's journey, you are welcome here." We say this not because we are friendly and nice. We say this because we *are* expanding our ecumenical vision, and we honestly believe that God is calling us to be one—not just one church, but one people in a world of increasing diversity. Amen.

Further Discussion: How does the United Church of Christ continue to proclaim its understanding of the "oneness" of humanity before God? From your knowledge of UCC history (both pre- and post-1957), what are our theological roots for embracing unity and diversity within worship, social action, spiritual education, and ecumenical partnerships?

Afterword

A member of First Church of Christ UCC in Hartford, Connecticut, Amy Ogden Welcher was elected the first president of the United Council of Church Women, an organization founded in 1941 with women from 70 denominations. I met "Miss Amy" in 1991, 50 years after her election. She was 104 years old, frail in body, but still filled with a fierce pride in the work of women in the church. "Women," she said, "always need to get outside of themselves and focus on what they can do for others." As the first president of UCCW, she pushed the organization to take initiative. People remembered her enthusiastic confidence in women and her admonition, "When in doubt, accelerate."

Barbara Brown Zikmund, "Church Women United," *Past as Prologue*. May 13, 2004 (ucc.org).

A Celebration of UCC Women

When the women who followed Jesus went to the tomb on that first Easter morning, they were doing two things: they were expressing their love and care for Jesus, and they were performing tasks women were expected to perform in that culture, preparing the body of the deceased for proper burial. As we celebrate the story of United Church of Christ women over 2,000 years later, we are very much like those women. We participate in the legacy of thousands of Christian women who have loved and cared for Jesus by sharing the good news of his coming and his empowering promises. And we also value and affirm the strength of all women who do what women should and can do in their traditional cultural circumstances. It is good that we do this.

The story of Easter morning is our story in still another way. We know that when those women got to the tomb, it was a disturbing experience. The stone was rolled away; two messengers asked them why they were looking for the living among the dead. At first they were confused, distraught, and frightened. "They bowed their faces to the ground." But gradually they came to remember what Jesus had told them about his future, how he

Barbara Brown Zikmund, "A Celebration of UCC Women," *New Conversations* Volume 4/Number 1 (Spring 1979), ed. Theodore H. Erickson. The article reprinted a speech given by BBZ at the "First National Meeting of UCC Women for Leadership Development," held in Cincinnati, Ohio, January 10–13, 1979, with 1,240 attendees.

would be crucified and rise. Revitalized, they immediately returned to tell the other disciples the good news. But, the scripture says, when the women announced that Jesus was risen, these words seemed to the disciples an idle tale, and they did not believe them. One recent translation says that the disciples considered the news to be "pure nonsense." Who would believe that a message of this magnitude would be carried by women? But God's ways are not bound by human expectations. It is a delight to remember that the Easter faith was shared first by women, even as it is painful to realize how quickly they were ignored and discredited.

Yet, this too is our story. Christian women throughout the centuries have been blessed and filled with news of the Christ, only to be discounted and ridiculed by established authorities. We have been telling our idle tales in many places where no one believed. Part of the history we share is a painful pattern of questioned credibility and thwarted mission. Any celebration, therefore, of women's discipleship dare not distort the record. Our joy is tempered with realism. We remember with indignation and sorrow, and we believe that it is important to remember.

For out of the complete story, we are empowered for mission. We rediscover the strength of Mary who accepted the creative potential within her and announced (as we have done) that her soul could magnify the Lord and her spirit would rejoice in God her savior.

We are creatures of the God who does not depreciate women's gifts or devalue women's status. In creation woman is co-equal with man. The biblical imagery from Genesis celebrates the unity of humanity in the ancient manner, by explaining that *woman* was created out of Adam. This language does not mean that woman is secondary, or derivative, but that she is truly human—so fully human that the *man* (not the woman) leaves his parents to cleave to her and "they become one flesh." This is a graphic Hebraic way of asserting the shared created perfection of humanity. Although later, human circumstances change and the injustices of inequality are laid upon sinful creatures, at the beginning God saw *everything* that was made, and behold, it was very good.

So, I begin my message to you by affirming our creation, by acknowledging our creativity, and by accepting the entire scope of our story. It is an impossible task, which I have embarked upon. But it is also a grace-full journey.

The story of UCC women, past and present, I have divided into seven chapters. . . . There could be six groups, or nine groups, but I choose to lift up seven ways that Christian women, especially United Church of Christ women, have lived their faith. I invite you to join me in our journey—remembering that parts of it are painful; that the people we find are among us, not above or ahead of us; and that their faces are our faces.

I.

Women in American church history have played a special role. Indeed, we have shaped the very nature of the American church as a voluntary organization by sharing our gifts through women's societies, guilds and fellowships. *The first women we celebrate, therefore, are the women who keep our churches alive.* Women who gather in groups to share the faith. Women who save and make money to sustain the faithful. Women who do "church work" and make it the work of the Lord. *Let us remember sharing women.*

It is important to realize that special women's organizations in our churches date from the beginning of the nineteenth century. They came into being because women accepted a personal obligation to share the faith and made a commitment to give one cent a week for Christian mission. Female societies for missionary purposes, or "female cent societies" as they were often called, argued that any woman could give one cent a week "if she denied herself some little thing." It is significant that the origin of women's organizations in our church was rooted in our Christian concern for others and not for ourselves.

Throughout the nineteenth century there were many women's boards for world and home mission. These local and regional women's aid societies, or missionary unions, gradually consolidated in the Congregational-Christian and Evangelical and Reformed churches. By the 1940s, women's work in our two antecedent denominations was directed through The National Women's Fellowship of the Congregational-Christian Churches and The Women's Guild of the Evangelical and Reformed Church. And with the creation of the United Church of Christ in the 1960s, still different national structures were created to support women's work (in the context of all lay activities) through the Council for Lay Life and Work.

With the gift of hindsight, it is easy to say that our national and egalitarian efforts to assimilate women's work into the regular program of the church were a mistake. Women lost that special ownership of outreach they had felt through the fellowship and the guild. They lost control over their money. Although it was a nonsexist vision which seemed to make theological sense, many women eventually felt betrayed.

. . . Our legacy from those early cent societies is the "Family Thank Offering." Church women in our history insisted that Christian living involved a daily awareness of God's blessings through prayer and giving. They developed a pattern of regularly setting aside small amounts of money which were especially dedicated as the "women's gift" or "women's thank offering." These monies were considered above and beyond regular church support. They were expressions of gratitude to be used in special ways. Since 1962, this tradition has found form in the yearly UCC Family Thank Offering. . . .

Some women have been disturbed that here in Cincinnati, [where the "First National Meeting of UCC Women for Leadership Development" was held January 10–13, 1979], we are spending this offering on ourselves. That is true. But we do ourselves a disservice if we discredit this gathering. We are here as instruments for the work of Christ's church. With "heart and mind" we are here to be sharpened and refined to do God's work. We are here called to go forth empowered for mission and justice. We are sharing women.

II.

Second, we celebrate women who extended the important role of Christian wife and mother to share their faith as educators. In the past when church women focused their energies and moved to exercise special leadership in our churches, they often became teachers. First, they taught their own families the faith. Then, they taught the children of unchurched neighbors. Soon women established and ran schools around the world. *Let us remember these teaching women.*

Early in colonial history, many organizations were founded to promote Christian knowledge and education. By 1825 a number of Bible and tract societies worked to spread Christian literature in our expanding nation. Women played key roles in these developments. Although the Sunday School movement began in England as early as 1781, after the organization of the American Sunday School Union in 1824, many women became deeply committed to Christian education. Women asserted their right to prepare themselves for teaching. Women combined their concern for abolition and education to serve as teachers for freed slaves in schools established by the American Missionary Association. Women in the Christian conference went forth to teach First Nations children in nearby tribes. Black women discovered their capacity as educators and led other Afro-Americans to freedom through education in Canada and later in the south. Hundreds of Christian women saw their unique calling to classrooms around the world.

Within the churches, women accepted the education of children and young girls as their responsibilities. A specialized form of church leadership emerged, particularly attractive to women: the director of Christian education or religious education. Women sought advanced training and credentials for this role. It was, and is, an important way for women to work in the United Church of Christ.

But this story has its painful aspects also. As Christian education became a woman's job, it was often devalued. In recent times the trend towards assistant or associate ministers of education has squeezed many vary capable women out of their jobs. Efforts to upgrade and remove sexist assumptions about leadership positions in our churches have complicated the situation. But we are still teaching women. If our children will have faith, we must raise them up in the ways of the Lord. If as sisters around the world women are to find freedom and justice, we must teach each other; not that our way is better, but that our God has blessed us. We are *teaching women.*

III.

Third, we celebrate women who accepted and created special opportunities to serve the church as missionaries and deaconesses. When American Protestantism launched its crusade to take Christianity around the world, women were essential to the success of mission work with thousands of women and children in distant places. When our internal frontier moved West and American Protestantism responded to the problems of health and social welfare created by urban growth, women were key leaders in the development of hospitals and homes for the orphaned and elderly. *Let us remember these serving women.*

The story of women on mission assignments has a special place in church history, because in mission work women's gifts were more than supportive to male ministry; women were essential to serve other women and children. In the cultures of the Near East and the Far East, where many women were protected and limited in all contact with men outside of their families, only missionary women were able to serve effectively and reach out to large sectors of the population. Early women missionaries, first as missionary wives and later as single women, founded and ran Christian schools for girls to combat the ignorance and powerless position of women in these lands. Women missionaries recognized the need for adequate health care and the ways that cultural taboos kept women from seeking the medical help of male doctors. They established clinics and hospitals for women and children, thereby reducing the dangers of childbirth and lowering infant mortality.

In all of these tasks, missionary women actually exercised more independent leadership in foreign fields than their stay-at-home sisters could manage in our local churches. It is not surprising, therefore, that some of the strongest and most able Christian women of the nineteenth and early twentieth century made a lifetime commitment to missionary work. Although their Christian enthusiasm bordered on cultural imperialism at times, we cannot slight the sincerity of their ministry or the importance of their leadership.

On the home scene, women also sought new ways to serve the church as it struggled to meet the changing needs of our expanding urban nation. These women were especially concerned to raise the quality of life among immigrant groups. They called for better medical care and more humane treatment of orphans. They worried about how people were going to take care of themselves when they got old.

Building upon the experience of German churches, some American denominations began to argue for a reclamation of the ancient order of the deaconess. By the 1880s, several groups moved to recognize and consecrate women for special work within and on behalf of the churches. And, between 1885 and 1900, almost 150 American deaconess institutions arose, all founded and sponsored by these "sisterhoods." Women in the Evangelical tradition of the United Church of Christ participated in this movement. By the early part of this century, they had established hospitals in Missouri, Illinois, Minnesota, Indiana, Ohio, Michigan, and Wisconsin. Deaconesses provided significant services to children's homes, to local churches, to settlement houses, and to the aged.

But this story has its upsetting feature also. The ironic journey of missionary women and deaconesses parallels that of other church women as we move closer to the present. When these women voluntarily turned to share the work of their institutions with men, and to consolidate their budgets into the mission of the general church, female leadership began to fade. Women's boards were not recruiting and supporting female missionaries. Women in the field did not have the same opportunities for training and leadership. Deaconesses could not escape a "second class" label. By the mid-twentieth century the unique calling and opportunities for women as missionaries and deaconesses were almost gone. But, in spite of these problems, we are their daughters. They accepted the mandate of the gospel and served their church. We, also, are *serving women.*

IV.

Fourth, we celebrate women who found themselves in ministry because of their marriage as much as their mission. These women accepted the trials implicit in their husband's call from the Lord. Many times, they sought out such a marriage in order to fulfill their personal call. *Let us remember supporting women.*

When Martin Luther married an ex-nun in the sixteenth century, he set forth a model for the parsonage family. Protestant clergymen from that time on into the present have leaned upon the strength of committed Christian partners. Congregations have assumed that their pastor's wife would have gifts and talents to enrich the work of her husband, so much so that our married clergymen often speak and write about their ministry as a family team. Some men would never survive the burdens of their role without this support. Certainly preachers' wives were the first assistant or associate pastors.

But we also know how unfairly the church has dealt with clergy wives. In unspoken ways, churches invaded privacy and took advantage of their love. These supportive ministries have been unnoticed, unappreciated, and unpaid. Yet women who married church leaders were expected to render special support . . . and most of us have done so with joy.

We are *supporting women.*

V.

Fifth, we celebrate women clergy. Although female leadership in our churches has existed in many forms, we take special delight in the capacity of women to accept a call to ordained leadership. In the pulpit and officiating at our Lord's table, women lead the Christian community towards a more egalitarian and androgynous future. It is particularly through preaching, which was rarely the major role of female educators, missionaries or deaconesses, that women clergy expand the power of women's ministries. *Let us remember these preaching women.*

From the colonial involvement of women in the "antinomian controversy" in Massachusetts, to the activities of women in our national crusade against slavery, proper etiquette prevented Christian women from public speaking before so-called "promiscuous assemblies" (audiences where both men and women were present). The growing participation of American women in the public sector, however, soon changed things. By the mid-twentieth century women sought theological training and ordination itself. The United Church of Christ takes great pride in the fact that a small Congregational church in upstate New York was the scene of the first ordination of a woman to the Christian ministry. The date was September 15, 1853.

It is significant that the sermon offered that day was entitled, "A Woman's Right to Preach the Gospel." For although many people would not object to female leadership in other facets of Christian ministry, they drew the line at preaching. The warning went out, "Beware of the petticoat in the pulpit." Is it surprising that women clergy today are so sensitive to the power of language in theology and the church? This is part of a continuing battle that women have had to uphold the credibility of their words and the integrity of *the* Word.

Even today, after many ordained women have broadened local expectations about ordained leadership in our churches, it is rare for a woman to be called as a senior preaching pastor in the United Church of Christ. And, if some women are denied opportunities to preach and bear testimony to their faith as ordained clergy, it becomes harder for all of us to proclaim the Word of the Lord. In an important way, we are enriched by *preaching women.*

VI.

Sixth, let us celebrate the emerging power and possibilities of women in diverse ethnic and racial traditions which are part of the United Church of Christ. These are women who find their roots in slavery. These are women whose people were here long before the "white man." These are women who mix East and West in a shrinking world. These are women who speak Spanish in our English-language environment. These are women who live in the social and political turmoil of so-called developing or third-world nations. *Let us remember emerging women.*

The common experience which binds these women together is the burden of oppression and the promise of liberation. These women have not had access to power in our world, but they have not languished in self-pity. In small and significant ways, they have led their people to freedom. They have claimed the justice of education. They have enriched the lives of their children. They have insisted that the gospel of Jesus Christ is not bound by the Anglo-Saxon mores of American life.

In the past many of these women have been invisible, lost in the distorted and peripheral vision of mainline Christianity. We do not even know their stories, and we weep when they are finally told; our tears flow as much for ourselves as for our sisters. These women chide us to keep the church honest. These women press us all on towards the radical implications of our faith. We are all *emerging women.*

VII.

And finally, seventh, let us celebrate the courage and ecumenical power of women who accept key leadership positions in the national and world church. Women who will not let their special offices and opportunities cause them to forget everyday faith and practice. Women who reconcile and heal the broken institutional church. *Let us remember leading women.*

Probably one of the most important expressions of female church leadership in this century is embodied in the formation of Church Women United. As women's associations, fellowships, boards, and guilds dissolved themselves into denominational structures, key leaders insisted that the worldwide network of women spawned by missionary work could not be lost. The

World Day of Prayer, started to support home and foreign missions in the 1880s, became the focal point for an international fellowship of Christian women. Its leaders celebrated the racial and ethnic mix of maturing church life throughout the world.

The pressures upon national church leaders are great. Sometimes it is difficult to remember that Christ's church exists in small villages as well as world assemblies. But women leaders are especially sensitive to the ambiguities of power and the price of success. They carry extra burdens in arenas of male dominance. We applaud these *leading women.*

Here is one overview of the creativity and the beauty of United Church of Christ women. We can drink from streams of living waters which flow from these seven pools of sisterhood. But we must not ignore the pain and the difficulties that can continue to rust our cups. We are the women of the United Church of Christ, past and present.

> We are *sharing women* who celebrate the power of women's work and organizations.
>
> We are *teaching women* who celebrate the tradition of Christian education.
>
> We are *serving women* who celebrate the gifts of missionaries and deaconesses.
>
> We are *supporting women* who celebrate the quiet contributions of clergy wives.
>
> We are *preaching women* who celebrate the importance of women clergy.
>
> We are *emerging women* who celebrate the possibilities of diverse racial and ethnic peoples.
>
> We are *leading women* who celebrate the opportunity to change the future of the church.

This is a legacy to inspire us and humble us. May our souls newly magnify the Lord and our spirits rejoice in God our savior. If we are willing to accept this legacy, let us respond with a joyous "Amen."

AMEN.

The Gospel of Luke tells us that through the healing power of Jesus Christ, the bent-over woman was able to stand straight and tall. The healing process which straightened her spine is a scripturally symbolic way of expressing the healing and wholeness which we would desire for all of God's children. But the bent-over woman is more than a generalized symbol of oppression, as powerful as that image may be. She is also a woman. And she reminds us of the particular call the Church has to address the question of injustices toward women.

Coordinating Center for Women (CCW)'s 1987 report to General Synod. Quoted by Barbara Brown Zikmund in "Celebrating the Memories: Selected Stories about Women and the United Church of Christ (1957–2007)," Local Church Ministries 2006.